THE PRIVATE DINING ROOM AND OTHER NEW VERSES

OGDEN NASH

The Private Dining Room

And other new verses

BOSTON

LITTLE, BROWN AND COMPANY

*Published simultaneously
in Canada by McClelland and Stewart Limited*

PRINTED IN THE UNITED STATES OF AMERICA

FOR NELL
THE ONLY GRANDCHILD
IN THE WORLD

Some of these verses first appeared in the following magazines and are reprinted through the courtesy of *Vogue, Good Housekeeping, Look, Flair, House and Garden, Harper's, The Saturday Evening Post, What's New, Glamour, The New Yorker, Life, Cosmopolitan* and *Woman's Day.*

CONTENTS

The Private Dining Room 3

Peekaboo, I Almost See You 5

Correction: *Eve* Delved and *Adam* Span 6

My Trip Daorba 8

The Anniversary 9

All, All Are Gone, the Old Familiar Quotations 11

Everybody Loves a Bride, Even the Groom 13

The Happy Ending of Mr. Train 15

The Calendar-Watchers, or, What's So Wonderful About Being a Patriarch? 17

I'm a Pleasure to Shop for 19

A Caution to Hillbilly Singers, Harpists, Harpoonists, Channel-Swimmers, and People First
in Line for World Series Tickets 21

A Caution to Everybody 22

Flow Gently, Sweet Etymology, Ornithology, and
Penology 23

The Snake, Without Whom Adam Would Never
Have Looked at the Lady Once 24

Shoo, Shoo, Shoemaker 25

I Didn't Say a Word, or, Who Called That
Piccolo Player a Father? 26

There's a Law, Isn't There? or, I Can Call You
Names But Don't Call Me Names 28

Calling Spring VII–MMMC 30

Everybody's Mind to Me a Kingdom Is, or,
A Great Big Wonderful World It's 32

Next!   34

They Won't Believe, on New Year's Eve, That
    New Year's Day Will Come What May   35

Change Here for Wichita Falls, or, Has Anybody
    Seen My Wanderlust?   36

Don't Look for the Silver Lining, Just Wait for It   38

Polonius, Yes, Polonius, No   40

The Astigmatic Naturalist
    THE CATERPILLAR   41
    THE TOUCAN   42
    THE PLATYPUS   43
    THE HAMSTER   44

With My Own Eyes   45

Two Goes into Two Once, if You Can Get It
    There   52

The Chef Has Imagination, or, It's Too Hard To
    Do It Easy   53

Why the Postman Has to Ring Twice, or, Yellow
    Envelope, Where Have You Gone?   55

The Wild Jackass   57

The Tortoise   58

The Aquarium   59

The Mules   60

The Cuckoo   61

The Birds   62

The Swan   63

The Voluble Wheel Chair   64

The Child Is Father to the Man, But with More
    Authority   66

The Visit   68

A Dog's Best Friend Is His Illiteracy   69

We Pause Now Briefly for an Important Message   71

Eheu! Fugaces, or, What a Difference a Lot of
    Days Make   73

Everybody Wants To Get into the Baedeker   75

Old Dr. Valentine to His Only Millionaire   77

Old Dr. Valentine to That Kind of Patient   78

Old Dr. Valentine to a Colleague   79

Old Dr. Valentine to His Son   80

Old Dr. Valentine for Once Dreams of Wealth   81

Roll Over and Play Alive, or, Who Says You
    Can't Teach an Old Dog Tiresome Tricks?   82

The Wendigo   84

Mr. Betts's Mind a Kingdom Is   85

The Strange Case of the Cautious Motorist   86

The Unwinged Ones   88

Whit Is Bibbidi-Bobbidi-Boo in Sanskrit?   90

You Can Be a Republican, I'm a Gerontocrat   92

Fables Bulfinch Forgot
    CHLOE AND THE ROUÉ   94
    THE THIRTEENTH LABOR OF HERCULES   96
    MEDUSA AND THE MOT JUSTE   98
    LEDA'S FORTUNATE GAFFE   100

Hi-Ho the Ambulance-o   102

Baby, It's Calder Inside   103

Everything's Haggis in Hoboken, or, Scots Wha
    Hae Hae   104

Father, Dear Father, Go Jump in the Lake, or, You're Costlier than You Think   106

Father-in-Law of the Groom   108

What's in a Name? Some Letter I Always Forget   110

Merry Christmas, You-All, or, Who Forgot Savannah?   112

The Strange Case of Mr. O'Banion's Come-Uppance   113

Hand Me Down the Old School Sliding Pads, or, There's a Hint of Strawberry Leaves in the Air   115

The Strange Case of the Lovelorn Letter Writer   117

Long Time No See, 'By Now   119

How To Get Along with Yourself, or, I Recommend Softening of the Oughteries   120

How High Is Up? A SORT OF CHANTEY   122

How To Be Married Without a Spouse, or, Mr. Kipling, What Have You Done with Mr. Hauksbee?   124

Have a Seat Behind the Potted Palm, Sir   126

Hey, Hey for the American Way   128

The Bat   129

The Chipmunk   130

The Grynch   131

Let's Not Play Lotto, Let's Just Talk   132

Tweedledee and Tweedledoom   133

I Remember Yule   134

Kipling's Vermont   136

M. C. Loves TV, or, A Personality Is Born   137

Max Schling, Max Schling, Lend Me Your Green
    Thumb

A TRAVELOGUE OF FLOWERY CATALOGUES   139

It's About Time   140

Maybe You Can't Take It With You, But Look
    What Happens When You Leave It Behind   142

Is It True What They Say About Dixie, or, Is It
    Just the Way They Say It?   143

The Club Car   144

Lecturer in Bookstore   145

The Dust Storm, or, I've Got Texas in My Lungs   146

Reflection on the Vernacular   147

I Can't Stop Unless You Stop, or, Lines Addressed
    to a Man Making $5000 a Year Who Overtips a
    Man Making $10,000 a Year To Make Himself
    Feel He's Making $20,000 a Year   148

You Can't Tell the Hit Parade Without a Drum
    Majorette   151

The Lepidopterist   153

This Is My Own, My Native Tongue   154

Love Me But Leave My Dog Alone   156

Limerick One   158

Limerick Two   159

Limerick Three   160

Just Press the Button, the Buttonhole Is Really
    a Deepfreeze   161

It Was Not I Who Posed for Rodin, or, Why I
    Flunked Philosophy IV   162

Tune for an Ill-Tempered Clavichord   164

THE PRIVATE DINING ROOM AND OTHER NEW VERSES

Miss Rafferty wore taffeta,
Miss Cavendish wore lavender.
We ate pickerel and mackerel
And other lavish provender.
Miss Cavendish was Lalage,
Miss Rafferty was Barbara.
We gobbled pickled mackerel
And broke the candelabara,
Miss Cavendish in lavender,
In taffeta, Miss Rafferty,
The girls in taffeta lavender,
And we, of course, in mufti.

Miss Rafferty wore taffeta,
The taffeta was lavender,
Was lavend, lavender, lavenderest,
As the wine improved the provender.
Miss Cavendish wore lavender,
The lavender was taffeta.
We boggled mackled pickerel,
And bumpers did we quaffeta.
And Lalage wore lavender,
And lavender wore Barbara,
Rafferta taffeta Cavender lavender
Barbara abracadabra.

Miss Rafferty in taffeta
Grew definitely raffisher.

Miss Cavendish in lavender
Grew less and less stand-offisher.
With Lalage and Barbara
We grew a little pickereled,
We ordered Mumm and Roederer
Because the bubbles tickereled.
But lavender and taffeta
Were gone when we were soberer.
I haven't thought for thirty years
Of Lalage and Barbara.

Middle-aged life is merry, and I love to lead it,

But there comes a day when your eyes are all right but
your arm isn't long enough to hold the telephone
book where you can read it,

And your friends get jocular, so you go to the oculist,

And of all your friends he is the joculist,

So over his facetiousness let us skim,

Only noting that he has been waiting for you ever since
you said Good evening to his grandfather clock
under the impression that it was him,

And you look at his chart and it says SHRDLU
QWERTYOP, and you say Well, why SHRD-
NTLU QWERTYOP? and he says one set of
glasses won't do.

You need two,

One for reading Erle Stanley Gardner's Perry Mason
and Keats's "Endymion" with,

And the other for walking around without saying Hello
to strange wymion with.

So you spend your time taking off your seeing glasses to
put on your reading glasses, and then remembering
that your reading glasses are upstairs or in the car,

And then you can't find your seeing glasses again because without them you can't see where they are.

Enough of such mishaps, they would try the patience of
an ox,

I prefer to forget both pairs of glasses and pass my de-
clining years saluting strange women and grandfather clocks.

CORRECTION: EVE DELVED AND ADAM SPAN

The ladies of the garden club
Are in the other room,
And, fed on tea and sandwiches,
Their pretty fancies bloom.
I hear their gentle treble hubbub,
The ladies of the garden clubbub.

The ladies of the garden club,
Their words are firm and sure,
They know the lore of lime and mulch,
The poetry of manure.
Each spring they beautify our suburb,
The ladies of the garden cluburb.

Dear ladies of the garden club,
I love your natural zeal,
Your verdant thumbs, your canvas gloves,
The pads on which you kneel,
But I hear you making plans involving
Husbands in gardening instead of golfing.

Between the outer door and me
The flower ladies sit.
I'm frantic-footed, blind, and trapped,
Like mole in compost pit,
One timorous masculine minutia,
Caught between baby's-breath and fuchsia.

The air is sweet with talk of bulbs,
And phlox and mignonettes;
Arrangements drape the drawer that holds
My only cigarettes.
Would I had courage for an end run
Round herbaceous border and rhododendron!

Ranunculus can a prison make,
And hyacinth a cell;
I barely glimpse a patch of sky
Through wreath of immortelle.
And thus are fulfilled the baleful prophecies
Concerning men who are at home instead of their offices.

I have just returned from a foreign tour,

But ask me not what I saw, because I am not sure.

Not being a disciplinarian like Father Day,

I saw everything the wrong way,

Because of one thing about Father Day I am sure,

Which is that he would not have ridden backwards so
that the little Days could ride forwards on their
foreign tour.

Indeed I am perhaps the only parent to be found

Who saw Europe, or eporuE, as I think of it, the wrong
way round.

I added little to my knowledge of the countryside but
much to my reputation for docility

Riding backwards through ecnarF and ylatI.

I am not quite certain,

But I think in siraP I saw the ervuoL, the rewoT leffiE,
and the Cathedral of emaD ertoN.

I shall remember ecnerolF forever,

For that is where I backed past the house where etnaD
wrote the "onrefnI," or ydemoC eniviD, and
twisted my neck admiring the bridges across the
onrA reviR.

In emoR I glimpsed the muroF and the nacitaV as in
a mirror in the fog,

While in ecineV I admired the ecalaP s'egoD as beheld
from the steerage of an alodnoG.

So I find conditions overseas a little hard to judge,

Because all I know is what I saw retreating from me as
I rode backwards in compartments in the niart and
in carriages sitting on the taes-pmuj.

THE ANNIVERSARY

A marriage aged one
Is hardly begun;
A fling in the sun,
But it's hardly begun;
A green horse,
A stiff course,
And leagues to be run.

A marriage aged five
Is coming alive.
Watch it wither and thrive;
Though it's coming alive,
You must guess,
No or yes,
If it's going to survive.

A marriage aged ten
Is a hopeful Amen;
It's pray for it then,
And mutter Amen,
As the names
Of old flames
Sound again and again.

At twenty a marriage
Discovers its courage.
This year do not disparage,
It is comely in courage;
Past the teens,

And blue jeans,
It's a promising marriage.

Yet before twenty-one
It has hardly begun.
How tall in the sun,
Yet hardly begun!
But once come of age,
Pragmatically sage,
Oh, blithe to engage
Is sweet marri-age.

Tilt a twenty-first cup
To a marriage grown up,
Now sure and mature,
And securely grown up.
Raise twenty-one cheers
To the silly young years,
While I sit out the dance
With my dearest of dears.

Who was born too soon? I will tell you who was born
    too soon: Francis Bacon, Baron Verulam.
Therefore he could not ask his friends, Why is Charles
    Lamb like Baltimore, and supply his own answer,
    Because he is deep in the heart of Mary Lamb.
Who was born too late? I will tell you without further
    parley:
It was I, because I cannot remember whether it was
    Charles Lamb or who, who on the death of his last
    nearest and dearest pathetically exclaimed, Now
    there is no one left to call me Charlie.
I am always getting entangled in such mnemonic snarls,
But from internal evidence it was obviously someone
    named Charles,
So it couldn't have been Scrooge or Marley.
Nor could it have been Charles II, because there was al-
    ways somebody to call him Charlie.
It would have been duck soup or pie or jam
If he had said, There is no one left to call me Elia,
    then I would have known it was Lamb.
If I could but spot a conclusion, I should race to it,
But Charles is such a simple name that I can't put a
    face to it.
Still, I shouldn't complain, since it is its simplicity that
    gives it its pathos;
There would be no poignancy in saying, There is no one
    left to call me Charlemagne or Lancelot or Athos.

People prefer the simple to the grandiose,
And I do not believe that even in an antique land anybody would sympathize with anybody who went
   around saying, There is no one left to call me
   Ozymandias.

EVERYBODY LOVES A BRIDE,
EVEN THE GROOM

Blessings on the bonnie bride,
I gaze upon her starry-eyed.
Brides are girls on whom I dote,
They bring a lump into my throat.
At the sound of Mendelssohn and Wagner
My spirit swoops like a tobogganer.

Beneath the shimmering bridal veil
Tomboys look demure and pale,
Hoydens turn into paragons,
And downy ducklings into swans.
I wish the Archbishop of Westminster
Would make a bride of every spinster.

Bless the bravely trousseau'd wife
Honeymooning into life.
Instead of showers of shoes and rice
Let us give her good advice.
Give it, and quickly dodge aside —
Have you ever tried to guide a bride?

Dear bride, remember, if you can,
That thing you married is a man.
His thoughts are low, his mind is earthy,
Of you he is totally unworthy;
Wherein lies a lesson too few have larnt it —
That's the reason you married him, aren't it?

The organ booms, the procession begins,
The rejected suitors square their chins,
And angels swell the harmonious tide
Of blessings upon the bonnie bride.
But blessings also on him without whom
There would be no bride. I mean the groom.

THE HAPPY ENDING OF MR. TRAIN

Once there was a man named Mr. Train who wasn't
called Choo-choo, which in itself is odd.

Furthermore, he knew a Mr. Rhodes who wasn't called
Dusty, and a Mr. Sloan who wasn't called Tod.

And they felt very unpopular not to be called Tod and
Dusty and Choo-choo,

Because this was back in the days when if you were
popular you were called Stinky or Baldy or the
Tennessee Shad, and chicle had just replaced to-
bacco as the new chew.

Well, of their unpopularity they grew wearier and
wearier,

Until they got together and decided that they were unpopular because they were superior,

And Mr. Sloan was asked by Mr. Rhodes, and Mr.
Train, who kept going CHOO-choo, CHOO-choo,
CHOO-choo, choo-CHOO,

Just how superior are YOU?

And Mr. Sloan replied that even as a child he had been
familiar with Homer's Iliad and Xenophon's Ana-
basis,

And he knew that the classical word for a clump of trees
was coppice, so that he always went over the river
and into the clump of trees to play coppice and rob-
berses,

And Mr. Rhodes and Mr. Train said You are still unpopular and alone,

You are not Tod, or even 's Liniment, you are still just
Mr. Sloan.

And the aesthetic Mr. Rhodes boasted, I am superior
    because to my fiancée who to marry me was waiting
    until I got a steady job I said It's not too good, it's
    truly too bad you waited,
Because I did have a steady job teaching Art for seven
    years, but Art just graduated.
And Mr. Sloan retired at once to his coppices and bosky
    abodes,
Murmuring, No Dusty he, nor even the Colossus of, he
    was born, lived, and will die, as Mr. Rhodes.
But Mr. Train, he ain't say nuffin'
Just set on de sidin', a-tootin' and a-puffin'.

THE CALENDAR-WATCHERS

or

WHAT'S SO WONDERFUL ABOUT BEING
A PATRIARCH?

I'm like a backward berry
Unripened on the vine,
For all my friends are fifty
And I'm only forty-nine.

My friends are steeped in wisdom,
Like senators they go,
In the light of fifty candles,
And one on which to grow.

How can I cap their sallies,
Or top their taste in wine?
Matched with the worldly fifties,
What chance has forty-nine?

Behold my old companions,
My playmates and my peers,
Remote on the Olympus
Of half a hundred years!

These grave and reverend seniors,
They call me Little Man,
They pat my head jocosely
And pinch my cheek of tan.

Why must I scuff my loafers
And grin a schoolboy grin?

Is not my waist as ample?
Is not my hair as thin?

When threatened with a rumba,
Do I not seek the bar?
And am I not the father
Of a freshman at Bryn Mawr?

O, wad some pawky power
Gie me a gowden giftie,
I'd like to stop at forty-nine,
But pontificate like fifty.

Mine is a dauntless spirit, meaning a spirit that is
   hard to daunt;
Therefore, since nobody gives me Christmas presents
   any more, I shall console myself by compiling a list
   of Christmas presents that I do not want.
I do not want a lamp made out of an umbrella stand, or
   a coffee table made out of an old wagon wheel, or
   a fire screen made out of a leftover piece of trellis,
Or, indeed, anything made out of, or to look like, anything ellis.
I do not want a novel written by a young genius in the
   earnest belief that nothing awful has ever happened
   before to anyone but him, certainly not to us dowdy
   duffers and stodgy codgers,
Nor tickets to the new musical by the smart boys who
   think they have discovered the secret of Hammer-
   stein and Rodgers.
Since I am crazy about harshness and unpleasant after-
   taste, I do not want a milder, less irritating cigarette, no matter how scientific the tests,
Nor an evening with friends watching the TV personality girls whom I can only think of irreverently as
   Community Chests.
I do not want a squirrel tail or a Confederate flag to
   dangle from the aerial of my car,
Or a picture window through which better to view my
   neighbor's picture window or the adjacent abattoir.
For me, please, no bottled Martinis,

No sweetbreads, no cottage cheese with or without
    chives, no blinis in sour cream, indeed, neither sour
    cream nor blinis.
If you will just not come across with any one of the
    above, and make it snappy,
You will also make one dear old gentleman's Christmas
    very, very happy.

A CAUTION TO HILLBILLY SINGERS,
HARPISTS, HARPOONISTS, CHANNEL–
SWIMMERS, AND PEOPLE FIRST IN LINE
FOR WORLD SERIES TICKETS

Fame was a claim of Uncle Ed's,
Simply because he had three heads,
Which, if he'd only had a third of,
I think he would never have been heard of.

Consider the auk;
Becoming extinct because he forgot how to fly, and
    could only walk.
Consider man, who may well become extinct
Because he forgot how to walk and learned how to fly
    before he thinked.

FLOW GENTLY, SWEET ETYMOLOGY, ORNITHOLOGY, AND PENOLOGY

Pronounce the Nightingale in Persian;
It comes out Bulbul in their version.
Thus every convict in Iran
Feels kinship with some Ossining man,
For be it summer-sing or spring-sing,
He loves to hear the Bulbul sing sing.

THE SNAKE, WITHOUT WHOM ADAM
WOULD NEVER HAVE LOOKED AT
THE LADY ONCE

Girls cry, upon the sight of snakes,
Faugh, Ugh, also, For heaven's sakes!
Thus many, many boys get kissed,
Which, without snakes, they might have missed.

SHOO, SHOO, SHOEMAKER

I often grieve for Uncle Hannibal
Who inadvertently became a cannibal.
He asked Aunt Mary to roast him the gobbler;
She understood him to say, the cobbler.

I DIDN'T SAY A WORD

or

WHO CALLED THAT PICCOLO PLAYER
A FATHER?

A man could be granted to live a dozen lives,
And he still wouldn't understand daughters and wives.
It may be because sometimes their ears are pierced for
     earrings,
But they have the most eccentric hearings.
Their hearings are in fact so sensitive
That you frequently feel reprehensitive.
At home, for instance, when near you,
Nobody can hear you.
After your most brilliant fireside or breakfast-table chats
     you can count on two fingers the responses you will
     have got:
Either, Don't mumble, dear, or, more simply, What?
I suppose if you're male and parental
You get used to being treated mental,
But you'd feel less psychically distant
If they weren't so inconsistent,
Because if you open your mouth in a hotel or a res-
     taurant their eardrums quiver at every decibel,
And their embarrassment is almost, if not quite, inex-
     precibel.
Their eyes signal What's cooking? at you,
And their lips hiss, Shush, Daddy, everybody's looking
     at you!
Now, I realize that old age is a thing of beauty,

Because I have read Cicero's De Senectute,
But I prefer to approach senility in my own way, so I'll
    thank nobody to rush me,
By which I mean specifically that my voice in a tearoom
    is no louder than anybody else's, so why does every-
    body have to shush me?

THERE'S A LAW, ISN'T THERE?

or

I CAN CALL YOU NAMES BUT DON'T CALL ME NAMES

Of obligations, by far the solemnest
Burden the conscientious columnist.
The world lies on his volcanic shoulders;
Sometimes he flames, sometimes just smolders.
Each morn he expounds to me and you
Just what we ought to think and do,
Or explains to us, by the setting sun,
Exactly what we ought to have done.
Besides the citizens and the nation,
He has another obligation —
The syndicated right divine
To keep other columnists in line.
Then who can blame him for his temper
When people continue so sic semper?
So go it, Westbrook,
And go it, Drew,
Tallyho, yoicks, and view halloo!

How the hide and the ivory fly about
When two bull columnists fall out!
One of them stepped on the other's feet,
He was eastbrook-bound on a westbrook street,
And, before you could say Louella Parsons,
There were libels and barratries, torts and arsons.
Only the Times continued to fiddle

While civilization split down the middle,
While kegler spat upon brother kegler,
Senior for Pearson, cadet for Pegler,
While millions of millions of plain pe-ople,
From Canada to Constantinople,
Held their breath, and followed each shot,
And wondered who would settle for what.

Then go it, Westbrook,
And go it, Drew,
Tallyho, yoicks, and view halloo!
It's like when Stalin
Was feuding Hitler,
Just — excuse the expression —
A little bit littler.

As an old traveler, I am indebted to paper-bound
    thrillers,
Because you travel faster from Cleveland to Terre Haute
    when you travel with a lapful of victims and killers.
I am by now an authority on thumbprints and finger-
    prints and even kneeprints,
But there is one mystery I have never been able to solve
    in certain of my invaluable reprints.
I am happily agog over their funerals, which are always
    satisfactorily followed by exhumerals,
But I can't understand why so many of them carry their
    copyright lines in Roman numerals.
I am just as learned as can be,
But if I want to find out when a book was first pub-
    lished, I have to move my lips and count on my
    fingers to translate Copyright MCMXXXIII into
    Copyright 1933.
I have a horrid suspicion
That something lies behind the publisher's display of
    erudition.
I may be oversensitive to clues,
But I detect a desire to obfuscate and confuse.
Do they think that because a customer cannot translate
    MCMXXXIII into 1933 because he is not a classi-
    cal scholar,
He will therefore assume the book to have been first
    published yesterday and will therefore sooner lay
    down his XXV cents or I/IV of a dollar?

Or do they, straying equally far from the straight and
    narrow,
Think that the scholarly will snatch it because the
    Roman copyright line misleads him to believe it
    the work of Q. Horatius Flaccus or P. Virgilius
    Maro?
Because anybody can make a mistake when dealing with
    MCMs and XLVs and things, even Jupiter, ruler of
    gods and men;
All the time he was going around with IO he pro-
    nounced it Ten.

EVERYBODY'S MIND TO ME A KINGDOM IS

or

A GREAT BIG WONDERFUL WORLD IT'S

Some melodies are popular as well as classical, which I
    suppose makes them popsicles,

And some poems are part William Cullen Bryant and
    part Nick Kenny which makes them thanatop-
    sicles,

And to some people Wisconsin is what Guinevere was
    to Launcelot,

And if they are away from it they are Wisconsolate.

Some naturalists know why the sphinx is sphinxlike and
    the griffin is griffiny,

And some couples are so wealthy that even their tiffs
    are from Tiffany.

Some Angeleno socialites fine each other a dollar

If they say La Jolla,

And give each other a Picasso or a Goya

For pronouncing it La Hoya.

Why should not I pick up a masterpiece or a coin?

I will no longer say Des Moines,

I shall sail into the C. B. & Q. ticket office like a
    swan,

And ask for a lower to Day Mwahn.

This I shall do because I am a conscientious man, when
    I throw rocks at sea birds I leave no tern un-
    stoned,

I am a meticulous man, and when I portray baboons I
    leave no stern untoned,

I am a man who values the fitness of things above notoriety and pelf,

Which is why I am happy I heard the cockney postmaster say to a doctor who was returning a leprechaun to Gloccamorra in an open envelope, Physician, seal thy h'elf.

NEXT!

I thought that I would like to see
The early world that used to be,
That mastodonic mausoleum,
The Natural History Museum.
Newspaper full of physicists,
I dropped my head upon my fists.
On iron seat in marble bower,
I slumbered through the closing hour.
At midnight in the vasty hall
The fossils gathered for a ball.
High above notices and bulletins
Loomed up the Mesozoic skeletons.
Aroused by who knows what elixirs,
They ground along like concrete mixers.
They bowed and scraped in reptile pleasure,
And then began to tread the measure.
There were no drums or saxophones,
But just the clatter of their bones,
A rolling, rattling carefree circus
Of mammoth polkas and mazurkas.
Pterodactyls and brontosauruses
Sang ghostly prehistoric choruses.
Amid the megalosauric wassail
I caught the eye of one small fossil.
Cheer up, old man, he said, and winked —
It's kind of fun to be extinct.

THEY WON'T BELIEVE, ON NEW YEAR'S EVE, THAT NEW YEAR'S DAY WILL COME WHAT MAY

How do I feel today? I feel as unfit as an unfiddle,
And it is the result of a certain turbulence in the mind
  and an uncertain burbulence in the middle.
What was it anyway, that angry thing that flew at me?
I am unused to banshees crying Boo at me.
Your wife can't be a banshee,
Or can she?
Of course, some wives become less fond
When you're bottled in bond.
My Uncle George, in lavender-scented Aunt Edna's day,
If he had a glass of beer on Saturday night, he didn't
  dare come home till the following Wednesday.
I see now that he had hit upon the ideal idea,
The passage of time, and plenty of it, is the only marital
  panacea.
Ah, if the passage of time were backward, and last night
  I'd been a child again, this morning I'd be fragrant
  with orange juice,
Instead of reeking of pinch-bottle foreign juice;
But if I should turn out to be a child again, what would
  life hold for me?
The woman I love would be too old for me.
There's only one solution to my problem, a hair of the
  dog, or maybe a couple of hairs;
Then if she doesn't get mad at me life will be peaceful,
  and if she does, it will show she really cares.

CHANGE HERE FOR WICHITA FALLS
or
HAS ANYBODY SEEN MY WANDERLUST?

Luxury travel is something for which I pant;
But who can afford it? The Aga Khan, and I can't.
Would I had studied Oriental languages as a pup;
I am always going to places where the timetable says
Read UP.
Trains that me back to ole Virginny or ole Indianny
carry,
They have always just dropped off the diner at Harris-
burg or Wilkes-Barre, which I always get confused
with John Wilkes-Barre.
Of streamliners and stratodomers I have heard gladsome
tidings,
But to me they are simply blinding streaks to make way
for which I have spent innumerable hours on rusty
sidings.
To some people travel conjures up a picture of luggage
plastered with glamorous labels and tags;
To me it is a picture of a remote station platform with
no porters and taxis, just me and my sacroiliac and
three heavy bags.
I am told that the comforts in modern hotels are stun-
ning;
My experience is that a hotel is a place with the ele-
vator out of order where you can only wash one
hand at a time because there is no stopper for the
drain and you have to keep squeezing the handles
of the faucet to keep the water running.

That is the hard way to get an ablution;

It reminds me of the visitor to the Chinese zoo who asked what language the aquatic carnivora talked, Pidgin English? and the keeper replied, No, Otter Confucian.

DON'T LOOK FOR THE SILVER LINING,
JUST WAIT FOR IT

The rabbit loves his hoppity and the wallaby loves his hippity.

I love my serendipity.

Let none look askance;

Serendipity is merely the knack of making happy and unexpected discoveries by chance.

Only yesterday I was bored by a bore — there is no topic that he isn't inept on it —

And when I pointed out a piece of chewing gum on the sidewalk, he was too busy talking to listen, so I soon made the happy and unexpected discovery that he had stepped on it.

It was serendipity when a recent hostess of mine in Philadelphia apologized for serving ham and eggs because she had forgotten to order scrapple,

Just as it was when I found a bow tie I could wear that didn't rise and fall with my Adam's apple.

I called it happy and unexpected when I found a funny paper with something funny in it,

And when I found a hole in my pocket but hadn't lost any money because I didn't have any money in it,

Also when I found a hole in my pocket which I had tickets for a harp recital in, or in which I had tickets for a harp recital, to put it properer,

So instead of the harp recital we had to see the Marx Brothers in A Night at the Opera.

If your coat catches on a branch just as you are about to
    slip over a precipice precipitous,
That's serendipitous,
But when you happily and unexpectedly discover that
    you don't have to go to the dentist or the chiropo-
    dist,
That's serendopitist.

I have always regretted that Hamlet slew Polonius,
With whom I think I would have got along very har-
monious.
Polonius said, "Neither a borrower nor a lender be,"
And that applies to me,
Because, as he continued, "loan oft loseth both itself
and friend,"
Which is grist for my mill, since I both have no credit
to borrow on and no loans to lend.
However, Polonius also said, "Costly thy habit as thy
purse can buy,"
Which is surely a personal matter between the little
tailor around the corner and I.
If I want to dress parsimonious,
What's that to Polonius?
My own rule of thumb is, "Costly thy raiment
As the first payment,"
But even had I the gold of Ophir,
I'd still feel entitled to go around wearing one wedgie
and one loafer.
Obviously Polonius was a busybody whom no snub
could embarrass,
So on second thought I don't regret that Hamlet stabbed
him behind the arras.

THE CATERPILLAR

I find among the poems of Schiller
No mention of the caterpillar,
Nor can I find one anywhere
In Petrarch or in Baudelaire,
So here I sit in extra session
To give my personal impression.
The caterpillar, as it's called,
Is often hairy, seldom bald;
It looks as if it never shaves;
When as it walks, it walks in waves;
And from the cradle to the chrysalis
It's utterly speechless, songless, whistleless.

The toucan's profile is prognathous,
Its person is a thing of bathos.
If even I can tell a toucan
I'm reasonably sure that you can.

I like the duck-billed platypus
Because it is anomalous.
I like the way it raises its family,
Partly birdly, partly mammaly.
I like its independent attitude.
Let no one call it a duck-billed platitude.

There is not much about the hamster
To stimulate the epigramster.
The essence of his simple story,
He populates the laboratory.
Then leaves his offspring in the lurch,
Martyrs to medical research.
Was he as bright as people am,
New York would be New Hamsterdam.

WITH MY OWN EYES

How often I've been overawed
By visiting lecturers from abroad,
Who glimpse our land in ten-day trips,
Between inbound and outbound ships,
Returning swiftly to their homes
To write encyclopedic tomes
Condemning all, not overlooking
Our wives, our culture and our cooking.

Of late, however, the foreign celebrity
Has yielded to native muliebrity,
By which ten-dollar phrase I mean
That lady lecturers stole the scene.
And how shall we distinguish, then,
The feminine speakers from the men?
The ladies have different architecture,
And make more money when they lecture.

But be they man or be they woman,
Lecturers have one trait in common;
For both the ladies and the gents
Seem to deplore their audience,
Wherefore they charge their hearers twice,
Their hearers pay a double price,
And double jeopardy they tote about;
First to be talked at, then to be wrote about.

How Fate on lecturers unleashes
Woes not unleashed on lesser species!

In return for money, plus expenses,
They suffer uncouth experi-ences.
What C.P.A. has come across
Raw oysters bathed in chocolate sauce?
What salesman roaming all the earth
Finds hedgehogs in his lower berth?

The greatest burden lecturers bear
Is meeting kindness everywhere.
Next year they black-list the locality
That shows the greatest hospitality,
For there is nothing that they hate
Like meeting those who pay the freight.
Successful ones insist their host
Shall treat them like the Holy Ghost.

Well, after this morose preamble,
I take a calculated gamble.
Remembering a recent trek
I venture to stick out my neck,
For I have hoisted on the platform
My tall, but in-the-middle-fat, form,
And purpose, if it please the court,
To file a minority report.

I do not claim, with ostentation,
That I have covered all the nation;
Still, for a freshman in the art,
I've made a reasonable start,
And lived in thirty-seven states

Through several hundred lecture dates.
Some people North and West and South
Don't know I ever close my mouth.

From Baltimore on the Chesapeake
I set out to speak and speak and speak.
I rode the Santa Fe and Pennsy,
And motored in S. C. and in N. C.,
And omnibused vertically, by gosh,
From Lewiston, I., to Pullman, Wash.
I learned that speaking brings on eczema,
And it's Yaki-ma, and not Ya-kima.

I've swallowed, in storms I near got lost in,
Dust in Texas and snow in Boston,
I've had waffle cookies in Fond du Lac,
And in Lincoln, a sacroiliac,
A token of Bryan's jealous wrath,
But I found an Omaha osteopath,
Thanks to whose ministrations fabulous
Neb. is to me no longer nebulous.

I've followed Northbound spring up hill
From Georgia to Jefferson's Charlottesville,
I've watched the garish Hollywood golfers,
And basketball at Gustavus Adolphus,
And on the shores of Puget Sound
The original theater in the round;
And be it anomalous, or analamous,
I've enlightened the scientists at Los Alamos,

· 47 ·

In Cleveland I've roamed Lake Erie's side,
Two full-fledged rabbis for my guide,
Baited professors without rebuke
Over a midnight-cap at Duke,
And in Florida, without a Collins,
Seen a president installed at Rollins.
I've seen the cypress and the yucca,
And a limestone statue of Joe Palooka.

Hardly among our current scarcities
Are colleges and universities;
So far I've visited ninety of them,
And, since they've been polite, I love them.
During the progress of my calls
On Quonset huts and ivied halls
I found no student and no dean
Resembling those upon the screen.

Colleges great and small I saw,
Chicago and Kent and Wichita,
Northwestern and Northern Idaho,
Washington, Pittsburgh, New Mexico,
Everywhere kids and G.I.'s together
Were chasing ideas, hell for leather.
Time has plowed under dear old Siwash;
The freshwater college jape is eyewash.

The noses in dust I'd like to rub
Of those who jeer at the woman's club.
They seem to deem male joiners manly,

Like Hemingway, Livingstone, and Stanley,
But should the women form in groups,
It proves them pretentious nincompoops.
Yet between Spokane and Grand Rapids
I noted a dearth of female Babbitts.

The ladies accept the rap unheeding
And quietly keep up their reading.
The members as well as Madam Chairman
Know Christopher Fry from S. N. Behrman;
They know Brancusi from St. Gaudens,
And Eliot's point of view from Auden's.
Some are even as handy with Greek and Latin
As any glamour girl in Manhattan.

I recently balked when I was looking in
A book that the author derided their cooking in,
Whose every chapter was all adrip
With peanut butter and marshmallow whip.
Why, before and after intoning ballads
I ate steaks and turkeys and plain green salads,
And from Sacramento to Cincinnati
I never caught sight of a chicken patty.

There's lots of land between the oceans,
And lots of people with lots of notions,
They're rural, and urban, and suburban;
They drink coffee, or coke, or Scotch, or bourbon;
And every region is proud to preach
Its way of life and way of speech;

Every state is a separate star,
With its own approach to the letter R.

The Middle West is doing nice
And doesn't need the East's advice;
It reads the Colonel for his comics,
Not for his theories on atomics.
The South may consign the North to Sheol
For confusing you-all with thou-all or thee-all;
But it seemed to me, from where I stood,
Our relations with us were pretty good.

Kansans, New Englanders, Carolinians
Stick to their ornery own opinions;
People don't swallow political prattle
With the single-mindedness of cattle;
People in overalls or mink
Are smarter than politicians think;
There is still a God's plenty left in people
Of the little red school and the tall white steeple.

I do not claim to be an oracle,
I state no statements categorical,
I'm just saying thanks for what I found
While I was wandering around.
Humility is a wholesome victual,
But why shouldn't the eagle scream a little?
If we differ on Truman or vivisection
We can always wait for the next election.

That the Stork is New York and America Billingsley,
Is a party line I'd follow unwillingsley,

So here's a thought which could be worser,
If you're East, look West, and vice versa.
The piano stretches from seaboard to seaboard;
Strike all the notes upon the keyboard.
The harmony rises, eagle-flighted,
The United States are still united.

TWO GOES INTO TWO ONCE, IF YOU
CAN GET IT THERE

All my life I have been a witness of things,

Among which I keep witnessing the eternal unfitness of things.

Daily it is my wont

To notice how things that were designed to fit each other, don't.

Getting a cigarette into a cigarette-holder is like the round hole and the square peg,

And getting the cork back into the vermouth bottle is like reinserting the cuckoo in the egg.

Why is the card-case always just a smidgin smaller than the deck?

Why does it take a 15¾ collar to encircle a 15½ neck?

Experience is indeed a teacher, and I have learned this fact from it,

That no suitcase is large enough to recontain the clothes you just unpacked from it.

No wonder the grapes set on edge the teeth of the little foxes;

The minute you buy a dozen silver or brocade or leather match-box holders the match-box makers change the size of the boxes.

I am baffled, I weave between Scylla and Charybdis, between a writ of replevin and a tort;

I shall console myself with the reflection that even in this world, ever perverse and ever shifting, two pints still make one cavort.

THE CHEF HAS IMAGINATION
or
IT'S TOO HARD TO DO IT EASY

Hark to a lettuce lover.
I consider lettuce a blessing.
And what do I want on my lettuce?
Simply a simple dressing.

But in dining car and hostel
I grow apoplectic and dropsical;
Is this dressing upon my lettuce,
Or is it a melting popsicle?

A dressing is not the meal, dears,
It requires nor cream nor egg,
Nor butter nor maple sugar,
And neither the nut nor the meg.

A dressing is not a compote,
A dressing is not a custard;
It consists of pepper and salt,
Vinegar, oil, and mustard.

It is not paprika and pickles,
Let us leave those to the Teutons;
It is not a pinkish puddle
Of grenadine and Fig Newtons.

Must I journey to France for dressing?
It isn't a baffling problem;

Just omit the molasses and yoghurt,
The wheat germ, and the Pablum.

It's oil and vinegar, dears,
No need to tiddle and toil;
Just salt and pepper and mustard,
And vinegar, and oil.

For Brillat-Savarin, then, and Hoyle,
Stick, friends, to vinegar and oil!
Yachtsman, jettison boom and spinnaker,
Bring me oil and bring me vinegar!
Play the music of Haydn or Honegger,
But lace it with honest oil and vinegar!
Choir in church or mosque or synagogue,
Sing, please, in praise of oil and vinegogue.
I'm not an expert, just a beginneger,
But I place my trust in oil and vinegar.
May they perish, as Remus was perished by Romulus,
Who monkey with this, the most sacred of formulas.

WHY THE POSTMAN HAS TO RING TWICE

or

YELLOW ENVELOPE, WHERE HAVE
YOU GONE?

Captain Ahab's desire was the White Whale.

My desire is to receive a telegram by telegraph messenger
and not by telephone or mail.

If I should be asked, What hath God wrought? by
Samuel F. B. Morse's ghost,

I should reply, He hath wrought the Telephone Company and the United States Post,

And I am still trying to read the riddle

Of how the Telegraph Company got that cozy seat in
the middle.

Oh Company uncertain, coy, and hard to please,

In the unprogressive olden times they relied on reliable
elderly boys with bicycles and puttees,

But now a telegram seems to be something that if
they can't mail it or phone it,

They disown it.

You stand convicted of impudence and effrontry

If you wish a telegram delivered, not mailed, to a person without a telephone in either the city or, what
they never heard of, the country.

Do not try to appease me, I am unappeasable,

For every time I send an important telegram to be per-
sonally delivered I am inevitably notified just too
late next day that delivery was impractical and
unfeasible.

Telegraph Company, you are the darling of my heart,
    I adore you,
In token of which I present you with a new slogan:
    Don't write, telegraph; we will mail it for you.

THE WILD JACKASS

Have ever you harked to the jackass wild,
Which scientists call the onager?
It sounds like the laugh of an idiot child,
Or a hepcat on a harmoniger.
But do not sneer at the jackass wild,
There is method in his hee-haw,
For with maidenly blush and accent mild
The jenny-ass answers, shee-haw.

THE TORTOISE

Come crown my brows with leaves of myrtle;
I know the tortoise is a turtle.
Come carve my name in stone immortal;
I know the turtoise is a tortle;
I know to my profound despair;
I bet on one to beat a hare.
I also know I'm now a pauper
Because of its tortley turtley torpor.

THE AQUARIUM

Some fish are minnows,
Some are whales.
People like dimples,
Fish like scales.
Some fish are slim,
And some are round.
Fish don't get cold,
And don't get drowned.
But every fish wife
Is jealous for her fish
Of what we call mermaids,
And they call merfish.

THE MULES

*In the world of mules
There are no rules.*

THE CUCKOO

Cuckoos lead Bohemian lives,
They fail as husbands and as wives,
Therefore they cynically disparage
Everybody else's marriage.

THE BIRDS

Puccini was Latin, and Wagner Teutonic,
And birds are incurably philharmonic.
Suburban yards and rural vistas
Are filled with avian Andrews Sisters.
The skylark sings a roundelay,
The crow sings "The Road to Mandalay,"
The nightingale sings a lullaby
And the sea gull sings a gullaby.
That's what shepherds listened to in Arcadia
Before somebody invented the radia.

THE SWAN

Scholars call the masculine swan a cob;
I call him a narcissistic snob.
He looks in the mirror over and over,
And claims to have never heard of Pavlova.

When you roll along admiring the view,
And everyone drives too fast but you;
When people not only ignore your advice,
But complain that you've given it to them twice;
When you babble of putts you nearly holed,
By gad, sir,
You are getting old.

When for novels you lose your appetite
Because writers don't write what they used to write;
When by current art you are unbeguiled,
And pronounce it the work of an idiot child;
When cacophonous music leaves you cold,
By gad, sir,
You are getting old.

When you twist the sheets from night to morn
To recall when a cousin's daughter was born;
When youngsters mumble and won't speak up,
And your dog dodders, who was a pup;
When the modern girl seems a hussy bold,
By gad, sir,
You are getting old.

When you scoff at feminine fashion trends;
When strangers resemble absent friends;
When you start forgetting the neighbors' names
And remembering bygone football games;
When you only drop in at the club to scold,

By gad, sir,
You are getting old.

But when you roar at the income tax,
And the slippery bureaucratic hacks,
And the ancient political fishlike smell,
And assert that the world is going to hell,
Why you are not old at all, at all;
By gad, sir,
You are on the ball.

THE CHILD IS FATHER TO THE MAN,
BUT WITH MORE AUTHORITY

Once there were some children and they were uninter-
ested in chores,
And they never picked anything up or put anything
back or brought anything in from out-of-doors.
They didn't want to take care of anything, just to play
with it,
And their parents let them get away with it.
Little did they know that Nemesis
Was on the premises.
Their regrets were at first scant
When they were left alone on their island summer
home because their parents were called away by the
convalescence of a wealthy aunt.
They prepared to take advantage of nobody being
around,
And this is what they found,
This is how they were hoist with their own petards,
There wasn't a deck with more than fifty-one cards,
And when they tried to play the handsome phonograph
with which they were equipped,
The records were either lost, warped or chipped,
There were bows but no arrows, and bats and gloves
but no ball,
And the untethered rowboat had drifted beyond recall,
And when they were wet the only towels were those
strewn on the bathroom floor where moisture lin-
gers,

And when they were cold they couldn't light a fire because all the matches had been used by people seeing how far down they would burn without burn-
ing their fingers.
Such experiences certainly taught them a lesson, and
when their parents returned to their native heath,
Why, the first thing these children did was to leave the
window open so it rained in on the piano, and go
to bed without brushing their teeth.

THE VISIT

She welcomes him with pretty impatience
And a cry of Greetings and salutations!
To which remark, no laggard, he
Ripostes with a Long time no see.
Recovering her poise full soon,
She bids him Anyhoo, sit ye doon,
And settling by the fireside,
He chuckles, Thank you, kind sir, she cried.
Snug as a bug, the cup he waits
That cheers but not inebriates.
She offers him a truly ducal tea,
Whipped up, she says, with no diffewclty.
A miracle, if I didn't know you,
He says — It only shows to go you.
Eying her o'er the fragrant brew,
He tells her her smile is picturescue,
And now he whispers, a bit pajamaly,
That he's fed to the teeth with his whole fam damily,
Perhaps she'll forgive an old man's crotchet
And visit Bermuda on his yachat.
She says she might, despite Dame Rumor,
Because he is a who than whom none is whomer.
He sidles close, but no cigar —
Until the yachat, au reservoir.

A DOG'S BEST FRIEND IS HIS
ILLITERACY

It has been well said that quietness is what a Grecian
    urn is the still unravished bride of,
And that a door is what a dog is perpetually on the
    wrong side of.
I may add that a sachet is what many a housewife's
    linen is fragrantly entrusted to,
But that a cliché is what a dog owner must eventually
    get adjusted to.
Whether your visitor be Mr. Belvedere or Bennett Cerf,
    what does he say when your dog greets him with
    Southern hospitality and salutes him all kissin'-
    cousiny?
He says, He smells my dog on me, doesn't he?
And he asks, How old is he, and you say Twelve, and
    he appraises Spot with the eye of an antiquarian,
And says, Seven twelves are eighty something, why
    Spot in human terms you're an octogenarian,
But these two bromides are just the rattle before the
    strike,
Because then he says it's funny but he's noticed how
    often dogs and their masters look alike.
Such are the comments faced by dog owners from
    Peoria to Peshawar,
And frequently from a man who in canine terms is 322
    years old, and he is the spit and image of his own
    Chihuahua.
The only escape is to have something instead of dogs

but whatever I substituted I should probably err,

And if I ended up with raccoons every guest would turn out to be a raccoonteur.

WE PAUSE NOW BRIEFLY FOR AN
IMPORTANT MESSAGE

To be grateful for small favors I am nothing loath,

Wherefore I have been recently counting my blessings, employing for the purpose the fingers of a three-toed sloth.

Blessing number one, although to appreciate it I am dilatory,

Is that as a child I was dropped chin-first into a barrel of depilatory,

So, not being that one man in seven who must shave every day, guess what I have never owned:

The precision razor equipped zip-twist with the sharpest edges ever honed.

I could never afford to own such a razor, because on TV I have seen with my own eyes that modern technology has made it so precise

That if you drop it once it gets all out of line and you can't use it twice,

You have to go out and buy a new precision razor right away,

And I know that between my tic and my palsy I would be in the market for a new precision razor at least every other day.

Blessing number two is that I didn't achieve my ambition to play for the Yankees or the Dodgers or the Giants

At least not since salesmanship has become a science.

Because think how it must add to a patriotic ballplay-
er's normal humiliation and regrets
To know that every time he doesn't complete a double
play or hit a home run some Veterans' Hospital
is deprived of six hundred less-irritating cigarettes.
Blessing number three is that though my head is now
considerably smaller than my waist
At least an advertising man is something I am not so
stupid as and as which I haven't got as bad taste.

or

WHAT A DIFFERENCE A LOT OF
DAYS MAKE

When I was seventeen or so,
I scoffed at money-grubbers.
I had a cold contempt for dough,
And I wouldn't wear my rubbers.
No aspirin I took for pains,
For pests no citronella,
And in the Aprilest of rains
I carried no umbrella.

When I was young I was Sidney Carton,
Proudly clad in a Spartan tartan.
Today I'd be, if I were able,
Just healthy, wealthy and comfortable.

When I was young I would not yield
To comforters and bed socks,
In dreams I covered center field
For the Giants or the Red Sox.
I wished to wander hence and thence,
From diamond mine to gold field,
Or piloting a Blitzen Benz,
Outdistance Barney Oldfield.

When I subscribed to The Youth's Companion
I longed to become a second D'Artagnan.

Today I desire a more modest label:
He's healthy, wealthy and comfortable.

When I was pushing seventeen,
I hoped to bag a Saracen;
Today should one invade the scene,
I'd simply find it embaracen.
Ah, Postumus, no wild duck I,
But just a waddling puddle duck,
So here's farewell to the open sky
From a middle-aged fuddy-duddle duck.

When I was young I was Roland and Oliver,
Nathan Hale and Simón Bolívar.
Today I would rather side step trouble,
And be healthy, wealthy and comfortuble.

EVERYBODY WANTS TO GET INTO
THE BAEDEKER

Most travelers eavesdrop
As unintentionally as autumn leaves drop,
Which brings up a question that confronts every con-
    scientious traveler:
Should he, or should he not, of overheard misinforma-
    tion be an unraveler?
The dear little old lady in front of you asks, What river
    is that, is it the Swanee or the Savannah?
And somebody who has no idea firmly says, It's the
    Potomac. It happens to be the Susquehanna.
The visiting Englishman asks, What is that mountain,
    and somebody yells, Pike's Peak! into his ear.
It isn't. It's Mt. Rainier.
Can one oneself of responsibility disembarrass
When one hears a fellow passenger being assured that
    the Île de France sails right up the Seine to Paris?
What is the etiquette
When one hears an eager sight-seer being informed that
    Greenwich Village is in Connecticut?
It is my experience that people who volunteer informa-
    tion are people who don't know the Eiffel Tower
    from the Tower of Pisa,
Or Desdemona from the Mona Lisa.
I am convinced that they have learned their geography
    through drawing mustaches on girls on travel
    posters,
And have done their own traveling exclusively on roller
    coasters.

What is that, madam? How do you get from 42nd
Street and Broadway to Times Square?

Sorry, madam, but it's impossible to get from here to
there.

OLD DR. VALENTINE
TO HIS ONLY MILLIONAIRE

I remember the shape you were in when you went
From the ambulance into the oxygen tent.
Your kidneys were clogged, your liver was leather;
I took you apart, then put you together.
I hear that today you're a Sedgman at tennis,
A Hogan at golf, and an amorous menace.
There's only one effort too much for you still:
To pick up your pen and pay my bill.

OLD DR. VALENTINE
TO THAT KIND OF PATIENT

During office hours I'm agog for your question,
Is it your heart, or indigestion?
But after your evening alcoholic
Of rye and champagne and lobster and garlic
When you phone me and wake me, I tell you flatly,
Please reverse the charges and call Clement Attlee.

OLD DR. VALENTINE
TO A COLLEAGUE

I have a patient's mother
Who hovers over me
And everything that I prescribe
That mother's bound to see.
She's read the Sunday papers
So she knows a hundred cures,
She knows more medicine than I,
And, Doctor, she is yours!

OLD DR. VALENTINE
TO HIS SON

Your hopeless patients will live,
Your healthy patients will die.
I have only this word to give:
Wonder, and find out why.

OLD DR. VALENTINE
FOR ONCE DREAMS OF WEALTH

Dr. Valentine hopes to announce
He's collecting fantastic amounts.
He's invented a bra
Called Peps-oo-la-la
Which delivers more bounce to the ounce.

ROLL OVER AND PLAY ALIVE

or

WHO SAYS YOU CAN'T TEACH AN OLD DOG TIRESOME TRICKS?

Brooks are often called rippling, but rivers are really
ripplinger,
And some writers are called Kipling when others are
Kiplinger,
And I understand that there was a turn-of-the-century
joke by which Mr. Kipling's surface was really
rippled:
ALGERNON: Do you like Kipling? SWEET YOUNG THING:
I don't know, I've never kippled.
I like making jokes, too,
But often it's so hard to make up my own that I take a
tip from radio and employ the switcheroo.
For years I led the conversation around to Missouri un-
til people got trapped into asking me how I liked
Joplin, and my, how their faces toppled
When I told them I had never joppled.
Now, alas, I must say farewell to my hardy-perennial
joke and pack it away in lavender and old poplin;
I have just been to, and been delighted with, Joplin,
And I have different ethics from a propagandizing Slav,
So how can I henceforth claim never to have joppled
when I really and truly have?
Which way to turn? I can as well imagine Southern
California agentless, or Little America snowless,
As me bon mot-less.

But hark, I hear the bugles of the switcheroo!
What works one time might as well work two.
I will imagine a jolly, untraveled Irish spinster,
One who has never seen either the Blarney Stone or
      Westminster,
And her friends Yeats and Synge and Lady Gregory,
      to make it a really name-worthy anecdote, ask her
      how she likes Dublin, and what does she say?
Well, the payoff follows as the night the day.

THE WENDIGO *

The Wendigo,
The Wendigo!
Its eyes are ice and indigo!
Its blood is rank and yellowish!
Its voice is hoarse and bellowish!
Its tentacles are slithery,
And scummy,
Slimy,
Leathery!
Its lips are hungry blubbery,
And smacky,
Sucky,
Rubbery!
The Wendigo,
The Wendigo!
I saw it just a friend ago!
Last night it lurked in Canada;
Tonight, on your veranada!
As you are lolling hammockwise
It contemplates you stomachwise.
You loll,
It contemplates,
It lollops.
The rest is merely gulps and gollops.

* WENDIGO: In the mythology of the northern Algonquians,
an evil spirit; one of a fabulous tribe of cannibals.

WEBSTER'S UNABRIDGED DICTIONARY

Do you know my friend Mr. Betts?
He claims he forgets.
When urged by Mrs. Betts to tell you about their trip
    to California he says he has no memory,
He is in a dilemma, he looks dilemmary.
He looks like a high-school music teacher substituting
    at the last minute for Iturbi,
And then he gives you a precise blow by blow, palm
    tree by palm tree, movie star by movie star ac-
    count, starting at the Grand Central and finishing
    with an appreciation of the waitresses' rear eleva-
    tion at the Brown Derby.
My friend Mr. Betts
Claims he forgets.
When asked by Mrs. Betts to tell you about that radio
    program that made her laugh, she thought she'd
    smother,
He says everything goes in one ear and out the other,
After which he takes the floor like Winston Churchill,
And re-creates the entire half hour from the first joke
    about the ungainly spinster who can't get a man
    to the final commerchill.

Do you know my friend Mr. Betts?
I wish I could remember as accurately as he forgets.

Have you read the biography of Mr. Schwellenbach?
    You can miss it if you try.

Mr. Schwellenbach didn't have much to live for, but
    he didn't want to die.

Therefore he was not only cautious, he was timid,

And if a savage-looking panhandler said to him, Gimme,
    he didn't call up the Better Business Bureau, he
    just gimmied.

Statistics of automobile fatalities filled his brain,

And he never drove over 25 miles an hour, and always,
    I regret to say, in the left-hand lane.

Whenever he stopped for a red light he cut off the ig-
    nition, put on the hand brake, locked all the
    doors, checked his license and registration cards,
    and looked in the glove compartment to see if he
    had mice,

So when the light turned green everybody behind him
    had to wait while he de-moused the car, reassured
    himself that he was driving legally, unlocked the
    doors, released the hand brake, reignited the igni-
    tion, pressed the wrong button and turned on
    Bing Crosby instead of the motor, and the light
    turned from green to red to green thrice.

Every autumn with the rains

Mr. Schwellenbach bought a new pair of chains.

He kept a record of every lethal blowout in the West-
    ern Hemisphere since 1921 in his files,

And he turned in his tires for new ones every 750 miles.

Well, he was driving on his new tires at 25 miles an
hour in the left-hand lane of a dual highway last
week, was Mr. Schwellenbach,

And a car coming the other way owned by a loan
shark who had bought his old tires cheap had a
blowout and jumped the dividing line and knocked
him to hellenbach.

THE UNWINGED ONES

I don't travel on planes.
I travel on trains.
Once in a while, on trains,
I see people who travel on planes.
Every once in a while I'm surrounded
By people whose planes have been grounded.
I'm enthralled by their air-minded snobbery,
Their exclusive hobnobbery,
And I'll swear to, before any notary,
The clichés of their coterie.
They feel that they have to explain
How they happen to be on a train,
For even in Drawing Room A
They seem to feel déclassé.
So they sit with portentous faces
Clutching their attaché cases.
As the Scotches they rapidly drain
That they couldn't have got on the plane,
They grumble and fume about how
They'd have been in Miami by now.
They frowningly glance at their watches,
And order more Scotches.
By the time that they're passing through Rahway
They should be in Havana or Norway,
And they strongly imply that perhaps,
Since they're late, the world will collapse.
Then, as station merges with station,
They complain of the noise and vibration.

These outcasts of aviation,
They complain of the noise and vibration.
Sometimes on the train I'm surrounded
By people whose planes have been grounded.
That's the only trouble with trains;
When it fogs, when it smogs, when it rains,
You get people from planes.

When people tell me French is difficult, I show my
dimple.

French is simple.

My pen is cosmopolitan, not parochial.

I am at home in French either classical or collo-
chial.

I can pronounce filet mignon even while chewing it,

And I can and will fluently translate popular songs such
as "Everybody's Doing It."

Tout le monde est faisant le, faisant le, faisant le,

Tout le monde est faisant le,

Faisant quoi?

Dindon pas!

Vois ce ragtime couple débonnaire,

Vois-les jeter leurs épaules en air,

C'est un hibou,

Un hibou, un hibou,

Où?

I think that even Mr. Berlin would agree that this has
life and movement,

And that the few changes are an improvement.

That ragtime couple, for example, instead of just being
vaguely over there,

They are now obviously in some expensive club, they
are debonair.

And the substitution of c'est un hibou, un hibou, un
hibou (it's an owl, it's an owl, it's an owl) for

c'est un ours, c'est un ours, c'est un ours (*it's a
bear, it's a bear, it's a bear*) —

That is a veritable coup de tonnerre,

That is a truly superior brand of merchandise,

Because in French ours (bear) might be confused with
oursin (sea urchin) and what would a debonair
owl-loving ragtime couple want with a fishy batch
of sea-urchindise?

I feel I have built myself a monument of more than
bricks and mortar,

And, having gained the gratitude of Mr. Berlin, I am
now leafing through the works of Mr. Oscar Ham-
merstein and Mr. Cole Porter.

YOU CAN BE A REPUBLICAN,
I'M A GERONTOCRAT

Oh, "rorty" was a mid-Victorian word
Which meant "fine, splendid, jolly,"
And often to me it has reoccurred
In moments melancholy.
For instance, children, I think it rorty
To be with people over forty.

I can't say which, come eventide,
More tedious I find;
Competing with the juvenile stride,
Or meeting the juvenile mind.
So I think it rorty, yes, and nifty,
To be with people over fifty.

The pidgin talk the youthful use
Bypasses conversation.
I can't believe the code they choose
Is a means of communication.
Oh to be with people over sixty
Despite their tendency to prolixty!

The hours a working parent keeps
Mean less than Latin to them,
Wherefore they disappear in jeeps
Till three and four A.M.
Oh, to be with people you pour a cup for
Instead of people you have to wait up for!

I've tried to read young mumbling lips
Till I've developed a slant-eye,
But all I can read, between the quips,
Is, if I can't, why can't I?
Oh, to be beside a septuagenarian,
Silent upon a peak in Darien!

They don't know Hagen from Bobby Jones,
They never heard Al Smith,
Even Red Grange is beyond their range,
And Dempsey is a myth.
Oh golly, to gabble upon the shoulder
Of someone my own age, or even older!

I'm tired of defining hadn't oughts
To opposition mulish,
The thoughts of youth are long long thoughts,
And Jingo! Aren't they foolish!
All which is why, in case you've wondered
I'd like a companion aged one hundred.

CHLOE AND THE ROUÉ

When Lord Byron wrote so glowingly of the isles of
    Greece

It was not mere coincidence or caprice.

Knowing his character and his environment,

I think we can guess what Lord Byron meant.

Nobody than Lord Byron could have been sorrier

About the death of a heroic Grecian warrior,

But nobody after so short a period

Could find consolation in the company of a nymph or
    a Nereid,

So all praise to the nymphs of the isles of Greece.

May their tribe increase.

But their tribe won't increase if they all behave like a
    nymph named Chloe,

Who lived on the southernmost isle of Greece where
    it is swampy, not snowy.

Chloe caught the attention of Zeus,

And he slipped away from the banquet hall mumbling
    some ridiculous excuse,

And when Hera called after him to come back, she
    knew what it meant when he got all skittish and
    scampery,

He said he'd be back for breakfast, he just had to see
    a mortal about a lamprey,

And he didn't want to tell a lie so he disguised himself
    as a lamprey fisherman but he couldn't find his
    lamprey-fishing clothes,

So aside from his lamprey-spear he was as naked as a
    narcissus or a rose,
And he tracked Chloe through the swamp and offered
    her his heart and a golden chariot, a dandy four
    wheeler,
But she refused because she was a Southern nymph, a
    Hellenic Dixiecrat, and she had been taught never
    to trust a nude eeler.

Some people think the nose of the Sphinx was flattened
    by Napoleon's cannoneers,
But it wasn't, not by several thousand years.
Credit should go to a person who dressed like Adam and
    talked like Pericles,
This person being known to us as Hercules and to the
    illiterate Greeks as Heracles,
And Hercules performed twelve fabulous labors,
Which caused all the inhabitants of Ultima Thule to ex-
    claim Begorra and Bejabers,
And just when he thought he was through with labors
    he was told by the gods, several of whom were his
    cousin,
That he must make it a baker's dozen.
They said that all brawn and no brain makes a dull
    demigod, so on immortality it was no dice
Unless he stumped the Sphinx thrice,
And Hercules said, Well I'll be a duck-billed platypus,
Here is a chance to avenge my friend Oedipus,
And he assumed an expression deceptively pleasant,
And he asked the Sphinx, Who is the heavyweight
    champion? and she said, Ezzard Charles, and he
    said, No it ezzant,
And he said, I'll give you another bone to pick at,
Why did Orpheus give up conducting and throw away
    his baton? and she said, I bet you don't know,
    either, and he said, Because there were more Bac-
    chantes than he could shake a stick at,

And the Sphinx said, You can't stump me three times in
a row, and he said, A house full, a hole full, you
cannot catch a bowlful, can you riddle me that
without straining?

And she said, Smoke? and Hercules said, No thank you,
I'm in training.

From that point

The Sphinx's nose has been out of joint.

Once there was a Greek divinity of the sea named Ceto
    and she married a man named Phorcus,

And the marriage must have been pretty raucous;

Their remarks about which child took after which parent
    must have been full of asperities,

Because they were the parents of the Gorgons, and the
    Graeae, and Scylla, and the dragon that guarded
    the apples of the Hesperides.

Bad blood somewhere.

Today the Gorgons are our topic, and as all schoolboys
    including you and me know,

They were three horrid sisters named Medusa and
    Euryale and Stheno,

But what most schoolboys don't know because they
    never get beyond their Silas Marners and their
    Hiawathas,

The Gorgons were not only monsters, they were also
    highly talented authors.

Medusa began it;

She wrote Forever Granite.

But soon Stheno and Euryale were writing, too, and
    they addressed her in daily choruses,

Saying we are three literary sisters just like the Brontës
    so instead of Gorgons why can't we be brontësau-
    ruses?

Well, Medusa may have been mythical but she wasn't
    mystical,

She was selfish and egotistical.

She saw wider vistas

Than simply being the sister of her sisters.

She replied, tossing away a petrified Argonaut on whom
she had chipped a molar,

You two can be what you like, but since I am the big
fromage in this family, I prefer to think of myself
as the Gorgon Zola.

The Greeks called the king of the gods Zeus and the
  Romans called him Jupiter.
Not that the Romans were stupider,
Jupiter being Roman for Zeus Pater, or Zeus the
  Father,
Which was appropriate, rather.
Zeus Pater is not to be confused with Walter Pater,
Who flourished later.
I don't even know if Walter Pater had a wife,
But I bet he never poured into a lady's room disguised
  as a shower of gold in his life.
Zeus Pater, on the other hand, was so eager to escape
  the restraint of his jealous queen that once he
  nearly killed a guard,
And in order to forward his unsavory amours he im-
  personated just about everybody except Hilde-
  garde.
One day he tiptoed out through heaven's portal
And picked up the handkerchief of a succulent
  mortal,
But when he wished to continue the acquaintance, he
  had run out of impersonations, he had nothing new
  to go as.
Juno always recognized him and followed him like Ruth
  after Boaz.
But this mortal happened to be Leda
And she was a great reader,
And when they were the equivalent of introduced,

Instead of Zeus, she thought the name was Proust,
And hey, hey!
The perplexing problem of what to impersonate was
  solved when she told him how much she admired
  Swann's Way.

People on wheels hate people on feet,
It takes two to make a one-way street.
Traffic commissions plan and study,
And nearly every is a body.

BABY, IT'S CALDER INSIDE

In addition to beauty and utility
The genuine mobile has mobility.
You know it's art when assorted metals
Caress your brow like falling petals.

EVERYTHING'S HAGGIS IN HOBOKEN

or

SCOTS WHA HAE HAE

That hero my allegiance earns
Who boldly speaks of Robert Burns.
I have an inexpensive hobby —
Simply not to call him Bobbie.
It's really just as easy as not
Referring to Sir Wally Scott,
But many, otherwise resolute,
When mentioning Burns go coy and cute.
Scholars hip-deep in Homer and Horace
Suddenly turn all doch-an-dorris;
Fine ladies who should pose and purr
Roll out a half-rolled Highland burr;
Conventioneers in littered lobby
Hoist their glasses in praise of Bobbie;
All, all Burns-happy and Bobbie-loopy,
They dandle him like a Scotian kewpie.
I'll brush away like gnats and midges
Those who quote from Bobbies Southey and Bridges;
I will not snap my Hopalong gun
At admirers of Bobbie Stevenson
(To be Bobbied is no worse, I guess,
Than being enshrined as R.L.S.);
I'd even attempt to save from drowning
Maidens who dream of Bobbie Browning;
Who refers to Bobbie Rossellini
Is just a harmless betwixt-and-betweenie;

I try to withhold my acid formic
From readers of Colonel Bobbie McCormick;
And I would not sink my knife to the haft
In supporters of Senator Bobbie Taft.
But of Robert Burns I'm a serious fan,
He wrote like an angel and lived like a man,
And I yearn to shatter a set of crockery
On this condescending Bobbie-sockery.
Well, I'm off, before I break the law,
To read Tommy Hardy and Bernie Shaw.

FATHER, DEAR FATHER, GO JUMP IN
THE LAKE

or

YOU'RE COSTLIER THAN YOU THINK

Once there was a man named Mr. Arents,
And he was the severest of parents.
Every time his seven children asked him when they
 could have a convertible he answered, bye and bye,
And he confiscated all their phonograph records that
 had songs with people singing, Aye yi aye yi.
He complained that they smoked too many cigarettes,
And he would neither feed nor bathe their pets.
He insulted all their friends at 4 A.M.
By standing at the head of the stairs in his pajamas and
 remarking, Ahem.
He insisted that they put on their shoes before they ate,
And objected when they scooped the middles out of the
 rolls and deposited the crust on their plate.
That was the erstwhile Mr. Arents,
The most unreasonable of parents.
You ought to see the new Mr. Arents,
He is a veritable model of forbearance.
He feels that whatever his seven children request,
It behooves him to behave at their behest.
Mr. Arents has had a warning,
Wherefore he brings them seven apples and seven con-
 vertibles each morning;
He is currying favor
Against the day his voice begins to quaver;

Any good will that his children may bear him, he wants
    to pad it,
He wants them to remember him as a right guy when
    he had it.
He knows that he is now an asset but he fears that all
    too soon
He will be an elderly liability in a chimney corner
    slurping porridge from a wooden spoon.
Mr. Arents has recently been told by an annuity sales-
    man something that makes him feel so singular that
    he has shrunk to Mr. Arent:
Namely, it is easier for one parent to support seven
    children than for seven children to support one
    parent.

Our times will be in books interred
As the era of the eaten word,
So tell me why should I alone
Be unprepared to eat my own?
The longer I live the sooner I find
How priceless is an open mind.
I trust that I am wiser plenty
At forty-nine than at nine and twenty.

How odd to think that once I rose
To sass my daughter's future beaux;
A new-born father, with arms akimbo,
Consigning all young men to limbo.
Since then I've lived a fifth of a century
Incredibly charming and adventury,
As you would have, were your vicinity
One of exclusive femininity.

For years I saw no male but me;
Even our Bedlington was a she.
I stood apart and watched agog
My wife, my daughter, and my dog.
They are a higher form of life,
My dog, my daughter, and my wife,
Inhabitants of a fourth dimension
Too mystic for my comprehension.

Life was a song in ancient Greece,
No debutantes disturbed the peace,
No sirens moaning o'er their hair

Left Mr. Paul for Mr. Pierre,
And ladies conscious of their backs
Avoided blue jeans, shorts, and slacks,
Yet alone among women, even Achilles
Got heebie jeebies and the willies.

Therefore I hail this happy anomaly,
A fellow male within the family,
And cause my daughter's wrath to bloom
By monopolizing of her groom.
Oh, let the girls get on with the trousseau
Here's a man Friday at last for Crusoe,
To chew the fat and exchange the dope with,
And a simple masculine mind to cope with.

A girl and her words are equally random,
No use to attempt to understand 'em.
You behold in me a crafty vet
Of Hoover's day and I'm trying yet.
But Johnny's talk is a green oasis
Of presidential and pennant races;
His forthright speech my mind relaxes
Even when discussing taxes.

Linell, though I can't read you clearly
You know I love you long and dearly.
You know I wish you barrel on barrel
Of joy and health and fine apparel,
And clinking corpulent piggy banks,
And please to accept my heartfelt thanks
For bringing me, my angel chile,
A man to talk to once in a while.

WHAT'S IN A NAME? SOME LETTER
I ALWAYS FORGET

Not only can I not remember anecdotes that are racy,
But I also can't remember whether the names of my
     Scottish friends begin with M-c or M-a-c,
And I can't speak for you, but for myself there is one
     dilemma with me in the middle of it,
Which is, is it Katharine with a K or Catherine with a
     C, and furthermore is it an A or is it an E in the
     middle of it?
I can remember the races between Man o' War and Sir
     Barton, and Épinard and Zev,
But I can't remember whether it's Johnson or Johnston
     any more than whether you address a minister as
     Mr. or Dr. or simply Rev.
I know a cygnet from a gosling and a coney from a
     leveret,
But how to distinguish an I-double-T from an E-double-
     T Everett?
I am familiar with the nature of an oath,
But I get confused between the Eliot with one L and
     one T, and the Elliot with two L's and one T, and
     the Eliott with one L and two T's, and the Elliott
     with two of both.
How many of my friendships have lapsed because of an
     extra T or a missing L;
Give me a simple name like Taliaferro or Wambsganss
     or Toporcer or Joralemon or Mankiewicz that any
     schoolboy can spell,

Because many former friends thought I was being im-
polite to them
When it was only because I couldn't remember whether
they were Stuarts with a U or Stewarts with an E-W
that I didn't write to them.

MERRY CHRISTMAS, YOU–ALL
or
WHO FORGOT SAVANNAH?

The men who draws the Christmas cards, dear,
They must have igloos in their yards, dear.
They lives in Labrador or Maine, dear.
They all knows how to harness reindeer.
They puts on snowshoes and galoshes,
And breaks the ice before they washes.

The men who writes the Christmas rhymes,
They all inhabits frigid climes.
Their roofs is fluffy, I have heared,
With snow like Santa Claus's beard.
Icicles decorate their nose,
And chilblains nips their mistletoes.

I loves the artists and the bards
Who makes the pretty Christmas cards,
I loves their winter scenes and such,
But still I thinks they don't know much,
For Christmas wanders back and forth
And travels South as well as North.

I'm glad our Christmas sun arises
On buttercups and butterflieses,
Our Christmas carol sounds as sweet
As if our ears was raw with sleet,
Our hearts is gay with Christmas mirth
Like on the colder parts of earth,
So cross the Mason-Dixon Line
And be my Christmas Valentine.

THE STRANGE CASE OF MR. O'BANION'S
COME-UPPANCE

Once there was a man named Mr. O'Banion,

And he was a depressing companion.

He was so cynical

That it was practically clinical.

He was also a skeptic,

And would never eat a hamburger without first immersing it in antiseptic.

He believed that actresses exist on amours and marijuana,

And that St. George's dragon was really a large iguana.

He stated that every man has his price,

And he was sure that bartenders use the same olive twice.

He was especially derisive of the names of summer cottages,

He said they stuck in his craws, of which he had developed two, and in his epiglottages.

He said there was nothing more fraudulent than a summer cottage's cognomen,

And one day he pointed out to his Scout troup that there were three large opaque billboards between Seaview Villa and the ocean, and that everybody was restless at Dunroamin.

He hinted that at Lilac Lodge you couldn't even raise dandelions, and scoffed that Mon Repos and Beau

Sejour would be the last place to find a French menu in,

And just as he remarked that Stuffed Sea Gull would be an apter name for Eagle's Eyrie, he was carried off by an eagle, and it was genuine.

HAND ME DOWN MY OLD SCHOOL
SLIDING PADS

or

THERE'S A HINT OF STRAWBERRY
LEAVES IN THE AIR

This is the outstretched, tentative toe,
The placid paddling into dotage:
To complement the radio
With the library of a summer cottage.

What calmer joy can life afford,
What more can fortune offer, or fame,
Than reading Mrs. Humphry Ward
While listening to the baseball game?

A glimpse of ducal silhouettes,
A flash of electronic science,
As kind hearts clash with coronets —
Also the Cardinals with the Giants.

The heroine's birth is most unusual —
It's three and two on Enos Slaughter.
What would she think of Stanley Musial,
And he of Lady Rose's daughter?

The code of stout King Edward's reign
Conceals outstanding hanky-panky,
Suggesting time and time again
The hidden ball of Eddie Stanky.

Beware, fair child of Lady Rose;
Warkworth, that cad, is far too cuddly!
Ah! Sure as Bobby Thomson's throws,
She's rescued by the Duke of Chudleigh!

In a world where even umpires err,
Why scorn the Duchess's stumbling start?
"When she learned at last he needed her,
The dear knowledge filled and tamed her heart."

Oh, bury me where the blue begins,
Where ball meets bat as lord meets lord,
Out where the home team always wins
And virtue is its Humphry Ward.

Dear Miss Dix, I am a young lady of Scandinavian
    origin, and I am in a quandary.
I am not exactly broody, but I am kind of pondery.
I got a twenty-five waist and a thirty-five bust,
And I am going with a chap whose folks are very upper-
    crust.
He is the intellectual type, which I wouldn't want to
    disparage,
Because I understand they often ripen into love after
    marriage,
But here I am all set
For dalliance,
And what do I get?
Shilly-shalliance.
Just when I think he's going to disrobe me with his eyes,
He gets up off of the davenport and sighs.
Every time I let down my hair,
He starts talking to himself or the little man who isn't
    there.
Every time he ought to be worrying about me,
Why, he's worrying about his mother, that's my mother-
    in-law to be,
And I say let's burn that bridge when we come to it,
    and he says don't I have any sin sense,
His uncle and her live in incense.
Well, with me that's fine,
Let them go to their church and I'll go to mine.

But no, that's not good enough for Mr. Conscience and
 his mental indigestion,
He's got to find two answers for every question.
If a man is a man, a girl to him is a girl, if I correctly
 rememma,
But to him I am just a high pathetical dilemma.
What I love him in spite of
Is, a girl wants a fellow to go straight ahead like a
 locomotive and he is more like a loco-might-of.
Dear Miss Dix, I surely need your advice and solace.
It's like I was in love with Henry Wallace.
Well, while I eagerly await your reply I'm going down
 to the river to pick flowers. I'll get some rosemary
 if I can't find a camellia.
Yours truly, Orphelia.

LONG TIME NO SEE, 'BY NOW

Let us all point an accusing finger at Mr. Latour.

Mr. Latour is an illiterate boor.

He watches horse racing, instead of the sport of kings,
when at the track,

And to him first base is simply first base, instead of the
initial sack.

He eats alligator pear instead of avocado,

He says fan, or enthusiast, instead of aficionado.

He has none of the feeling for words that Ouïda and
Spinoza felt,

Instead of Eleanor, he says Mrs. Roosevelt.

Sometimes he speaks even more bluntly and rashly,

And says the former Mrs. Douglas Fairbanks Senior, or
the ex-Mrs. Clark Gable, instead of Sylvia, Lady
Ashley.

He drinks his drinks in a saloon instead of a tavern or
grill,

And pronounces Know-how, skill.

He calls poor people poor, instead of underprivileged,

Claiming that the English language is becoming over-
driveleged.

He says the English language ought to get out of the
nursery and leave the toys room,

So he goes to the bathroom instead of the little boys'
room.

I will offer the hand of my daughter and half my income
tax to him who will bring me the head of Mr.
Latour on a saucer

Before he has everybody else talking as illiterate as
Defoe and Chaucer.

HOW TO GET ALONG WITH YOURSELF

or

I RECOMMEND SOFTENING OF THE OUGHTERIES

When I was young I always knew
The meretricious from the true.
I was alert to call a halt
On other people's every fault.
My creed left no more chance for doubt
Than station doors marked IN and OUT.
A prophet with righteousness elated,
Dogmatic and opinionated,
Once self-convinced, I would not budge;
I was indeed a hanging judge.
I admitted, in either joy or sorrow,
No yesterday and no tomorrow.
My summary of life was reckoned
By what went on that very second.
I scoffed when kindly uncles and aunts
Said age would teach me tolerance,
For tolerance implies a doubt
That IN is IN and OUT is OUT.
But now that I am forty-nine
I'm tolerant, and like it fine.
Since the faults of others I condone,
I can be tolerant of my own.
I realize the sky won't fall
If I don't pay my bills at all.
The King of Sweden it will not irk

To hear that I neglect my work,
And tombfuls of historic dead
Care not how late I lie abed.
Oh, tolerance is the state of grace
Where everything falls into place,
So now I tolerantly think
I could tolerate a little drink.

HOW HIGH IS UP?

A SORT OF CHANTEY

Yo heave ho!
Blow the man down, Johnny!
Yo heave ho!
Blow him out of town, Johnny!
Heave yo heave!
Gangway, stairway!
Heave yo heave!
Heave him on the airway!
Fly away, Johnny!
Fly, bonnie Johnny!

The last thing I remembers, I drunk with Deadeye Dick,
My throat is full of embers, and my tongue is tarnal
thick.
I gulps my penicillin for to clarify my brain,
And discovers I am shanghaied on a airyplane.

Oh, maybe I am headed for Cathay or Caroline;
God grant it ain't the corner of Hollywood and Vine!
They have battened down the hatches and I cannot
see a thing
But the high tension wires and a section of the wing.

Yo heave ho!
Feel the rudder wag, Johnny!
Yo heave ho!
Where's the paper bag, Johnny!

Heave yo heave!
Flying men is hardier!
Heave yo heave!
Gander and La Guardia!
Fly away, Johnny!
Fly, bonnie Johnny!

How Nature hastes to welcome the conqueror of space!
How fog and ice enclasp it in rapturous embrace!
This contraption is a triumph of man's inventive wit,
The very mountains skip like rams to get in front of it.

Oh, now the lordly agent, outbargaining the sun,
Can eat his lunch at Chasen's and dine at Twenty-one.
Who that has rode this comet of aluminum and ply-
        wood
Would prefer an upper berth behind a grimy choo-
        choo?
I would.

Yo heave ho!
Blow the man down, Johnny!
Yo heave ho!
Blow him out of town, Johnnyi
Heave yo heave!
Heave him in the stratosphere!
Heave yo heave!
Chesterfields they satisphere!
Fly away, Johnny!
Fly, bonnie Johnny!

HOW TO BE MARRIED WITHOUT
A SPOUSE

or

MR. KIPLING, WHAT HAVE YOU DONE
WITH MR. HAUKSBEE?

Do any of you old fogies remember Mrs. Hauksbee?
Without Mrs. Hauksbee, Simla and Poona
Would have been just like Altoona.
At Mrs. Hauksbee's burra khanas
Nabobs pinned tails on donkeys and viceroys bobbed
for bananas.
Mrs. Hauksbee disentangled subalterns and aides-de-
camp
From shopworn maids-de-camp.
Mrs. Hauksbee could rock India with one jab
In the Punjab.
Under the deodars, whatever they may be, Mrs. Hauks-
bee was in her glory,
But this is another story.
Mrs. Hauksbee was attended by a faithful old amah,
Which is the equivalent of in Alabama a faithful old
mamah,
And this now amah was a conservative reactionary
Hindu,
And she got tired of Mrs. Hauksbee all the time shifting
her hemline and her hair-do and her skin-do,
And finally she asked Mrs. Hauksbee why she had dyed
her hair again and she got one of the usual an-
swers.

Mrs. Hauksbee said she was changing her style to reform
young Slingsby of the Umpteenth Lancers,
And the amah (she had surreptitiously attended the
Sorbonne)
Murmured, "Plus ça change, plus c'est la memsahib,"
and wandered on.

HAVE A SEAT BEHIND THE POTTED
PALM, SIR

I'm just an untutored traveling man,
And I only know as much as I can,
But ask me about itineraries,
And I'll tell you one factor that never varies:
All of the overnight trains arrive
In the dim-lit neighborhood of five.
Wherever you come, from wherever you've gone,
You always get into town at dawn.
You're reluctant to sway to the washroom once more
Between quivering curtain and quavering snore;
Why should one, when one in one's pocket hath
A hotel reservation for room and bath?
Detroit, Seattle, Dubuque, New Haven,
You descend at sunrise unbuttoned, unshaven,
In yesterday's socks and yesterday's shirt,
And yesterday's city's pervasive dirt,
But only a jiffy, you fondly suppose,
From a bath and a nap and a change of clothes,
Seeing you hold what is laughingly termed
A hotel reservation, confirmed.
You approach the desk with footstep glad,
And your reservation ironclad.
The clerk offhandedly waves you aside;
Your room is there, but it's occupied.
No use to wheedle, nobody to placate;
You're marooned till the squatter decides to vacate.
You retire to a crowded bench in the lobby,

And pretend that your beard is a lovable hobby.
By noon you're a vagrant, offensive and jailable;
You're finally told that your room is available.
You ascend to your castle among the stars,
And what do you find? Four dead cigars,
Towels and sheets in a crumpled bunch,
And word that the maid is out to lunch.
By confirmed reservations I'm stymied and bunkered;
I'd just as soon trust a confirmed drunkard.

The Founding Fathers were men of outstanding talents,
And they founded our system of check and balance,
But you have to discover things before you can found
    them,
So they discovered the system of check and balance by
    looking around them,
Thus proving to their own satisfaction
That every action has its equal reaction.
Why do dog-owners grow thin?
Because a dog has to scratch the door to get out so he
    can turn around and scratch to get in.
Tit is always equal to tat,
And the hopeful relief of a family moving from a flat to
    a house is balanced by the hopeful relief of a family
    moving from a house to a flat.
Facts are things that there is no reply to them,
And it is a fact that the active bliss of greeting guests
    leads to the reactive bliss of saying good-by to them,
And that is why the Founding Fathers celebrated the
    discovery of action and reaction with a couple of
    beers or so,
And gave us the system of checks and balances in which
    the Republicans are equal to the Democrats, at
    least every twenty-four years or so.

THE BAT

Myself, I rather like the bat,
It's not a mouse, it's not a rat.
It has no feathers, yet has wings,
It's quite inaudible when it sings.
It zigzags through the evening air
And never lands on ladies' hair,
A fact of which men spend their lives
Attempting to convince their wives.

THE CHIPMUNK

My friends all know that I am shy,
But the chipmunk is twice as shy as I.
He moves with flickering indecision
Likes stripes across the television.
He's like the shadow of a cloud,
Or Emily Dickinson read aloud.
Yet his ultimate purpose is obvious. very:
To get back to his chipmonastery.

THE GRYNCH

I dearly love the three-toed grynch,
It grows upon me inch by inch.
Each home with one should be provided;
The Lord did not create it, so I did.
It's useful for closing conversations
With stubborn salesmen and poor relations.
Long-winded storytellers flinch
If I bring up the three-toed grynch.
When I speak of the grynch which I adore
I'm a bore, I'm a bore, I'm a fabulous bore.
But so can life be; in a pinch,
I recommend the three-toed grynch.

If anybody says conversation in our day is as good as it
    was in Dr. Johnson's,
Why, that's a lot of nonsense.
The art of conversation has been lost, or at least mislaid,
And no modern phrase-coiner can think of a fresher
    word for spade than spade.
Take the causerie of the most effervescent coterie,
It sounds like something sworn to before a notary.
Where are yesterday's epigrams, banter and badinage?
All you hear is who behaved scandalously at the club
    dance and how hard it is to get a new car into an
    old garage.
The maxim, the apothegm, yea, even the aphorism, die
    like echoes in the distance,
Overwhelmed by such provocative topics as clothes,
    beauticians, taxes and the scarcity of competent
    domestic assistants.
Come, sprinkle ashes and coffee substitutes upon my
    head,
I weep for the art of conversation, it is dead.
But wait a minute, the art of conversation is not dead,
    see it arise, vigorous, stimulating and untroubled,
Just as you start to play six spades, vulnerable, doubled
    and redoubled.

TWEEDLEDEE AND TWEEDLEDOOM

Said the Undertaker to the Overtaker,
Thank you for the butcher and the candlestick-maker,
For the polo player and the pretzel-baker,
For the lawyer and the lover and the wife-forsaker,
Thank you for my bulging, verdant acre,
Said the Undertaker to the Overtaker.
Move in, move under, said the Overtaker.

I guess I am just an old fogey.

I guess I am headed for the last roundup, so come along little dogey.

I can remember when winter was wintery and summer was estival;

I can even remember when Christmas was a family festival.

Yes, I can remember when Christmas was an occasion for fireside rejoicing and general good will,

And now it is just the day that it's only X shopping days until.

I can remember when we knew Christmas was coming without being reminded by the sponsor

And the annoncer.

What, five times a week at 8:15 P.M., do the herald angels sing?

That a small deposit now will buy you an option on a genuine diamond ring.

What is the message we receive with Good King Wencelaus?

That if we rush to the corner of Ninth and Main we can get that pink mink housecoat very inexpenceslaus.

I know what came upon the midnight clear to our backward parents, but what comes to us?

A choir imploring us to Come all ye faithful and steal a 1939 convertible at psychoneurotic prices from Grinning Gus.

Christmas is a sitting duck for sponsors, it's so commercial,

And yet so noncontroversial.

Well, you reverent sponsors redolent of frankincense and myrrh, come smear me with bear-grease and call me an un-American hellion,

This is my declaration of independence and rebellion.

This year I'm going to disconnect everything electrical in the house and spend the Christmas season like Tiny Tim and Mr. Pickwick;

You make me sickwick.

The summer like a rajah dies,
And every widowed tree
Kindles for Congregational eyes
An alien suttee.

or

A PERSONALITY IS BORN

I have one kindly kamerad, I have one true amigo,
Who made me what I am today, my supersonic ego.
I can't enjoy July the Fourth unless I'm Uncle Sam,
Ham that I am.
As Boston thinks of Bunker Hill, as Richmond thinks
    of Lee,
As Moscow thinks of Uncle Joe, that's how I think of
    me,
An unprecedented wow, like chlorophyll or Boulder
    Dam,
Ham that I am.
I shudder for my parents when I think that maybe
Instead of me they might have had some other baby.
I congratulated mother in a telegram,
Ham that I am.

When bothered by the common cold, the fever and the
    chills,
The common man takes aspirin, but I need wonder
    pills;
I shiver like Alaska, I perspire like Alabam,
Ham that I am.
I have a native courtliness that nothing can embarrass,
My accent when I eat at Child's transforms it into
    Paris,
I call the waiters garçon and the hostesses Madame,

Ham that I am.
I'm delighted with my country and I've often said it,
A nation that produced myself deserves much credit.
I'm the maraschino cherry in the cherrystone clam,
Ham that I am.

I wrote a lot of operas that were stolen by Puccini,
I wrote the Canterbury Tales while sipping a Martini,
I wrote The Rubáiyát and signed it Omar Khayyám,
Ham that I am.
Instead of simple business cards I've illustrated folders,
I keep a mermaid in my tub to scrub between my
    shoulders,
My taste is so developed I put caviar on jam,
Ham that I am.
It's obvious a genius of my wit and wisdom
Is called upon to entertain the Solar System.
Compared to me a Barrymore is just a bashful lamb,
Ham that I am,
That I am.

MAX SCHLING, MAX SCHLING, LEND
ME YOUR GREEN THUMB

A TRAVELOGUE OF FLOWERY CATALOGUES

Bobolink!
Bobolink!
Spink!
Spank!
Spink!
Bobbink!
Atkink!
Sprink!

Burpee.

How simple was the relationship between the sexes in
    the days of Francesca di Rimini;

Men were menacing, women were womeny.

When confronted with women, men weren't expected
    to understand them;

Their alternatives were, if rejected, to un-hand, if ac-
    cepted, to hand them.

I attribute much of our modern tension

To a misguided striving for intersexual comprehension.

It's about time to realize, brethren, as best we can,

That a woman is not just a female man.

How bootless, then, to chafe

When they are late because they have no watch with
    them, all eleven of their watches are on the dress-
    ing table or in the safe;

How fruitless to pout

When you can never follow the clues in your detective
    story because they believe that every time the dog
    scratches, it really wants to go out;

Bear it and grin

When having been silent all day they time their tele-
    phone calls to coincide with Groucho Marx and
    Ed Wynn;

Give your tongue to the cat

When you ask what they want for their birthday and
    they say, Oh anything, and you get anything, and
    then discover it should have been anything but
    that.

Above all, don't behave like a Monsieur Verdoux

Merely because after spending two hours arranging
themselves to attract you they don't want you to
succumb to their attraction because then you
would disarrange their lipstick or hairdo.
Pocket the gold, fellows, ask not why it glisters;
As Margaret Fuller accepted the universe, so let us
accept her sisters.
Women would I think be easier nationalized
Than rationalized,
And the battle of the sexes can be a most enjoyable
scrimmage
If you'll only stop trying to create woman in your own
image.

MAYBE YOU CAN'T TAKE IT WITH YOU, BUT LOOK WHAT HAPPENS WHEN YOU LEAVE IT BEHIND

As American towns and cities I wander through,
One landmark is constant everywhere I roam;
The house that the Banker built in nineteen-two,
Dim neon tells me is now a funeral home.

IS IT TRUE WHAT THEY SAY ABOUT DIXIE

or

IS IT JUST THE WAY THEY SAY IT?

Our country, South and West of Hatteras,
Abounds in charming feminine flatteras.
Sweet talk is scant by Lake Cayuga,
But in Tennessee, they chatta nougat.

Come, child, while rambling through the nation
Let's practice our pronunciation.
The liquid confluence here we see
Of r-i-b and a-l-d.
When first potato chips he nibbled,
That gentleman was merely ribald,
But now that he is four-rye-highballed,
We may properly pronounce him ribald.

LECTURER IN BOOKSTORE

Behold best-selling Mr. Furneval,
Behind a pile of books to autograph,
Like a bearded lady at a carnival
Hoping to sell her fly-specked photograph.

THE DUST STORM

or

I'VE GOT TEXAS IN MY LUNGS

Nobody minds
Dust storms in Lubbock;
They don't create havoc,
Just hubbubbock.
But I'm so full
Of Holy Texas
I'll be hallowed ground
When they annex us.

REFLECTION ON THE VERNACULAR

In cooking petits pois, or lesser peas,
Some use receipts, and some use recipes.
In spite of opposition warm,
I choose to use the former form.
In fact, though you may think me gossipy,
I plan to settle near Lake Ossipee,
When my arrangements are complete
To change its name to Lake Osseipt.

I CAN'T STOP UNLESS YOU STOP
or
LINES ADDRESSED TO A MAN MAKING $5000 A YEAR WHO OVERTIPS A MAN MAKING $10,000 A YEAR TO MAKE HIMSELF FEEL HE'S MAKING $20,000 A YEAR

I do not wish to tiptoe through the tulips to Tipperary,
And I might vote for Tyler too, but about Tippecanoe
    I am a little wary.
The fact is, that at any mention of any form of tips,
My mind goes into an eclipse.
The world of tips has moved too fast for me,
The price of ransoming my hat has become too vast
    for me.
I have to get used to one thing at a time,
And just as I learn that there is no more such tip as a
    nickel, I find that there is no more such tip as a
    dime.
If you give a dime to a bellhop,
The skyscrapers buck like broncos, and you can almost
    feel the hotel hop.
If you want to talk to bellhops or porters,
You start with baby-talk, which is quarters.
If you want to talk to head waiters, or, as they now
    style themselves, Maitre d's,
You talk in C's or G's,
And the girl with the tray of cigarettes expects the Taj
    Mahal,

And not a small Mahal, either, but a large Mahal.
This is a sad situation for low and middle income persons,
And when you go abroad, it worsens.
At least on the trains over here
You don't have to tip the conductor and the engineer,
And over here, certainly until recently, it would have been considered impudent effrontery
To tip the President of the country,
Whereas, in certain nations that shall be nameless,
The entire citizenry is shameless.
Granted that itching palms
Know no qualms,
Nevertheless people, whether men or mice,
Resent scratching the same palm twice,
Which happens wherever you eat or sleep, on the continent, because a fat percentage is added to the bill to cover all tips,
But if you think that no further tipping is expected, you'd better learn to carry your own pemmican and balance your baggage on your hips.
Oh dear, I think that extravagant tips are an unnecessary menace,
Whether in Valdosta, Georgia, or Valparaiso, or Vancouver, or Venice.
I think that they are a betrayal of the tipper's unsure ego, or not quite-quiteness,
I think that they are a vulgar substitute for common politeness.

I think that people could do very well both at home
   and abroad on moderate gratuities or fees
If they would just take the trouble to learn and employ
   the foreign and domestic terms for Thank you,
   and Please.

YOU CAN'T TELL THE HIT PARADE
WITHOUT A DRUM MAJORETTE

In Africa, it's the sirocco.
Our equivalent is the disc jocko.

The jocko's chatter is brisk,
Four commercials to every disc.

The commercials are Brahmses and Bachs
Compared to the discs he jocks.

For instance, he cannot assuage
His passion for Patti Page,

That perhaps too talented elf
Who sings quartets by herself.

Thanks to scientific genius,
She sings four parts simulteneous.

If snowbound alone on a ridge,
I suppose she could always play bridge,

But such multiple schizophrenia
Is a vocal misdemeanior.

Yet nothing delights the disc jocko
Like Patti's quadruple echo.

Her effect on disc jockos is radical,
Like blackstrap molasses or Hadacol;

They will even curtail their chatter
To spin you her recentest platter.

What will hold me through Patti and the commercial?
It's only my middle-aged inertia'll.

Thus grumbles this radio kibitzer,
But I doubt that I jolt the jock discers.
My opinions are flibberty-gibbertzer,
And Coolidge peeks out through my whiskers.

THE LEPIDOPTERIST

The lepidopterist with happy cries
Devotes his days to hunting butterflies.
The leopard, through some feline mental twist,
Would rather hunt a lepidopterist.
That's why I never adopted lepidoptery;
I do not wish to live in jeopardoptery.

Often I leave my television set to listen to my wireless,
So, often I hear the same song sung by the same singer
many times a day, because at repeating itself the
wireless is tireless.
There is one such song from which at sleepy time I can
hardly bear to part,
A song in which this particular singer, who apparently
has offended a nameless character in an undescribed
way, states that he apawlogizes from the bawttom
of his heart.
I am familiar with various accents — I know that in In-
diana you stress the "r" in Carmen,
And that in Georgia if a ladybug's house is on far she
sends for the farmen,
And I have paaked my caah in Cambridge, and else-
where spoken with those who raise hawgs and
worship strange gawds — but here I am, late in
life's autumn,
Suddenly confronted with somebody's apawlogies and
bawttom.
I tell you whawt,
Things were different when I was a tawddling tawt.
I may have been an indifferent schawlar,
Lawling around in my blue serge suit and doodling on
my Eton cawllar;
In fact, I didn't even pick up much knawledge
In a year at cawllege;

I guess that of normal intelligence I had only about two
    thirds,
But, by gum, I was taught, or, by gum, was I tot, to
    pronounce my words.
And now they've gawt me wondering:
Was it the dawn or the don that from China cross the
    bay came up thundering?
As a tot, was I tawddling or was I toddling?
When I doodled, was I dawdling or was I dodling?
I have forgawtten oll I ever knew of English, I find my
    position as an articulate mammal bewildering and
    awesome.
Would God I were a tender apple blawssom.

LOVE ME BUT LEAVE MY DOG ALONE

Once there was a handsome man named Mr. Beamington and he was to good causes the most generous
of donors,

And he was so popular with dogs that he couldn't understand why he was so unpopular with their owners.

He was bold as an eagle, a cock eagle, yet gentle as a
dove, a hen-dove,

And the dog didn't live that he couldn't make a friend
of.

If you had a brace of ferocious spaniels

Mr. Beamington would soon be romping with them
through your annuals and peranniels.

He fondled schnauzers

With no scathe to his trousers.

At his voice the pit bull eschewed the manners of the
bull pit,

And assumed those of the pulpit.

He could discuss Confucianism with a Pekinese,

And address the Boston terrier on Beacon Hill in purest
Beaconese.

Yes, Mr. Beamington had a way with dogs, dogs simply
adored him,

Yet their owners abhorred him,

Because he reckoned without the third law of Paracel-
sus,

Which clearly states that every dog-owner considers his
dog a one-man dog, and its affection his own and
nobody elsus.

So the only people who liked him were the owners of
    a Cairn,
Which frequently bit him, thus reassuring them that
    its heart was not hisn but theirn.

LIMERICK ONE

An elderly bride of Port Jervis
Was quite understandably nervis.
Since her apple-cheeked groom,
With three wives in the tomb,
Kept insuring her during the service.

There was a young lady of Guam
Who peddled her charms, charm by charm,
Inspired, I suppose,
By the classical prose
Of W. Somerset Maugham.

LIMERICK THREE

A lady from near Rising Sun,
She flattened her boy friend in fun,
Saying, Don't worry kid,
That's for nothing you did,
It's for something I dreamt that you done.

JUST PRESS THE BUTTON, THE BUTTON-
HOLE IS REALLY A DEEPFREEZE

You ask the cause, madam, of my agitation?
Gadgetation.
I am one who found sufficient duplicity
In plain old electricity;
Now that it has become electronics,
My vapors are chronics.
I am just a modest student of householdology,
Not a graduate of the Massachusetts or California In-
    stitutes of Technology.
Once I was master in my own home, and my family's
    hearts with pride went hippity-hoppit,
Because when the plumbing kept on running I knew
    how to lift the lid of the tank and twiddle with
    the ball, and stop it.
Today my satellites are rather less sycophantic than
    Saturn's
Simply because when I touch the television I get noth-
    ing but herringbone and sharkskin patterns;
I am no longer the Old Man, He Who Sees All and
    Knows All,
I am only He Who Put the Bubble Gum in the Dispose-
    All.
The scientists are so far out in front of each other that
    even my bedclothes croon,
Ignoring which, I shall put myself to sleep with my
    dog-eared copy of Tom Swift and His Wonderful
    Illuminating Gas Balloon.

IT WAS NOT I WHO POSED FOR RODIN

or

WHY I FLUNKED PHILOSOPHY IV

Once you really get thinking about thinking,
It's worse than drinking.
You begin to think that because you think, you
    exist,
And you proceed to think that anything not thought
    about by you has no more existence than the clench
    after you have unclenched your fist.
You become so involved in the spirit
That you think a noise is not a noise unless you are
    there to hear it,
And speaking of noise, by this time you are thinking so
    dreamily
That you think your voice when you listen to it in the
    bathtub rings out Wagnerianly, or at least Frimly.
Your id is now cooking with iridium;
You think that a couple of Martinis improve your
    French in both accent and idiom.
The only trouble is that the French have been thinking,
    too,
And they think faster than you,
Which they naturally have to by at least two thirds
Just to keep up with their own words,
Because you may be the language-ropin' champion of
    Texas, mah deah suh,
But still they can say, "Qu'est-ce que c'est que ça,"
    quicker than you can say, "Huh?"

Nevertheless, I think that nothing is but thinking makes
    it so,
And I intend to take two Martinis and sing "Frère
    Jacques" in my bath and think the French into
    talking slow.

TUNE FOR AN ILL-TEMPERED
CLAVICHORD

Oh, once there lived in Kankakee
A handy dandy Yankakee,
A lone and lean and lankakee
Cantankakerous Yankakee.
He slept without a blankaket,
And whiskey, how he drankaket,
This rough and ready Yankakee,
The bachelor of Kankakee.
He never used a hankakee,
He jeered at hanky-pankakee;
Indeed, to give a frank account,
He didn't have a bank account.
And yet at times he hankakered
In marriage to be anchachored.
When celibacy rankakles,
One dreams of pretty ankakles.
He took a trip to Waikiki
And wooed a girl named Psycheche,
And now this rugged Yankakee
'S a married man in Kankakee.
Good night, dear friends, and thankakee.

A lady from near Rising Sun   160
A man could be granted to live a dozen lives   26
A marriage aged one   9
All my life I have been a witness of things   52
An elderly bride of Port Jervis   158
As American towns and cities I wander through   142
As an old traveler, I am indebted to paper-bound
   thrillers   30

Behold best-selling Mr. Furneval   145
Blessings on the bonnie bride   13
Bobolink!   139
Brooks are often called rippling, but rivers are
   really ripplinger   82

Captain Ahab's desire was the White Whale   55
Come, child, while rambling through the nation   144
Come crown my brows with leaves of myrtle   58
Consider the auk   22
Cuckoos lead Bohemian lives   61

Dear Miss Dix, I am a young lady of Scandinavian
   origin, and I am in a quandary   117
Do any of you old fogies remember Mrs.
   Hauksbee?   124
Do you know my friend Mr. Betts?   85
Dr. Valentine hopes to announce   81
During office hours I'm agog for your question   78

Fame was a claim of Uncle Ed's   21

Girls cry, upon the sight of snakes   24

Hark to a lettuce lover   53
Have ever you harked to the jackass wild   57

Have you read the biography of Mr. Schwellen-
    bach?   86
How do I feel today? I feel as unfit as an unfiddle   35
How often I've been overawed   45
How simple was the relationship between the
    sexes in the days of Francesca di Rimini   140

I dearly love the three-toed grynch   131
I do not wish to tiptoe through the tulips to
    Tipperary   148
I don't travel on planes   88
I find among the poems of Schiller   41
I guess I am just an old fogey   134
I have a patient's mother   79
I have always regretted that Hamlet slew Polonius   40
I have just returned from a foreign tour   8
I have one kindly kamerad, I have one true amigo   137
I like the duck-billed platypus   43
I often grieve for Uncle Hannibal   25
I remember the shape you were in when you went   77
I thought that I would like to see   34
If anybody says conversation in our day is as good
    as it was in Dr. Johnson's   132
I'm just an untutored traveling man   126
I'm like a backward berry   17
In addition to beauty and utility   103
In Africa, it's the sirocco   151
In cooking petits pois, or lesser peas   147
In the world of mules   60
It has been well said that quietness is what a
    Grecian urn is the still unravished bride of   69

Let us all point an accusing finger at Mr. Latour   119
Luxury travel is something for which I pant   36

Middle-aged life is merry, and I love to lead it 5
Mine is a dauntless spirit, meaning a spirit that is
    hard to daunt 19
Miss Rafferty wore taffeta 3
Most travelers eavesdrop 75
My friends all know that I am shy 130
Myself, I rather like the bat 129

Nobody minds 146
Not only can I not remember anecdotes that are
    racy 110

Of obligations, by far the solemnest 28
Often I leave my television set to listen to my
    wireless 154
Oh, once there lived in Kankakee 164
Oh, "rorty" was a mid-Victorian word 92
Once there was a Greek divinity of the sea named
    Ceto and she married a man named Phorcus 98
Once there was a handsome man named Mr.
    Beamington and he was to good causes the
    most generous of donors 156
Once there was a man named Mr. Arents 106
Once there was a man named Mr. O'Banion 113
Once there was a man named Mr. Train who
    wasn't called Choo-choo, which in itself is odd 15
Once there were some children and they were
    uninterested in chores 66
Once you really get thinking about thinking 162
Our country, South and West of Hatteras 143
Our times will be in books interred 108

People on wheels hate people on feet 102
Pronounce the Nightingale in Persian 23
Puccini was Latin, and Wagner Teutonic 62

Said the Undertaker to the Overtaker 133
Scholars call the masculine swan a cob 63
She welcomes him with pretty impatience 68
Some fish are minnows 59
Some melodies are popular as well as classical,
   which I suppose makes them popsicles 32
Some people think the nose of the Sphinx was
   flattened by Napoleon's cannoneers 96

That hero my allegiance earns 104
The Founding Fathers were men of outstanding
   talents 128
The Greeks called the king of the gods Zeus and
   the Romans called him Jupiter 100
The ladies of the garden club 6
The lepidopterist with happy cries 153
The men who draws the Christmas cards, dear 112
The rabbit loves his hoppity and the wallaby
   loves his hippity 38
The summer like a rajah dies 136
The toucan's profile is prognathous 42
The Wendigo 84
There is not much about the hamster 44
There was a young lady of Guam 159
This is the outstretched, tentative toe 115
To be grateful for small favors I am nothing loath 71

When I was seventeen or so 73
When I was young I always knew 120
When Lord Byron wrote so glowingly of the isles
   of Greece 94
When people tell me French is difficult, I show
   my dimple 90
When you roll along admiring the view 64

Who was born too soon? I will tell you who was
    born too soon: Francis Bacon, Baron Verulam   11

Yo heave ho!   122
You ask the cause, madam, of my agitation?   161
Your hopeless patients will live   80